Build Trust
Create Loyalty
Deliver Outstanding Service

Michael Heppell

Sunday Times No.1 Bestselling Author

See, Smile, Say Hello

A CIP catalogue record of this book is available from the British Library.

First edition published in the UK by Gloop Books, 2025.

ISBN: 978-1-8381613-2-3 (Paperback)
Imprint: Gloop Books
Typeset: Matthew J Bird

For further information about this book, please contact the author:
www.MichaelHeppell.com

For Andy Alderson

A message from HIT Training

HIT Training are proud to offer this book – from Michael Heppell – as a companion resource for you as you undertake your learning journey with HIT Training and beyond. It will inspire, guide, advise, comfort and act as a lifelong reminder of this first step you have made to a bright future.

HIT Training partnering with Michael in shaping the future of the hospitality industry is an exciting journey – driven by a shared passion for excellence and a commitment to developing a world-class workforce.

In an era where customer expectations are higher than ever, delivering exceptional front-of-house service is no longer just an advantage; it's a necessity. Through training, mentorship, and hands-on expertise, we are equipping professionals with the skills to be not only flexible and adaptable but also polished and professional.

This collaboration is about more than just service it's about crafting experiences and ensuring that every guest interaction leaves a lasting impression. From hands-on workshops like 'The Art of Service' and 'Service Experience' to our innovative 'Hearts and Minds' learning interventions, we promise that each and every day will be insightful, challenging, inspiring and of course, fun!

The book alongside our hospitality industry training offer will support you in mastering front-of-house delivery, building confidence, and gaining the competitive edge that turns one-time visitors into lifelong patrons.

Contents

Introduction 11

See 19

1 See 21

2 The Personal Touch *When is a suit not a suit?* 22

3 The Cultural Lens 26

4 I Would Have Bought The Mercedes *Literally, See Me* 31

5 The Power Of Pain
What problem are you actually solving? 35

6 See Me *The Art Of Observation* 38

7 The Generation Game 45

8 Seeing And Being Seen 50

9 RADAR Thinking™ *In The Real World* 53

10 The Devil Is In The Detail 58

11 Convenient For Whom? *Why I'm not a fan of the scan* 62

12 Never Knowingly Underwhelmed 65

13 Sell Me More *Upselling with integrity* 67

Smile 75

14 Smile 77

15 The Science Of Smiling
Creating emotional connections 79

16 Confidence vs Arrogance 84

17 Trusting Your Gut
How to harness emotional intelligence 90

18 Malaga Eggs 93

19 Laughing Together
The power of humour in customer service 98

20 Creating A Positive Environment
The real reason to smile 103

21 Trust Me: *I'm A Customer Service Expert* 107

22 It's Not You, It's Me 110

23 Loyalty 4.0 114

24 No Bad Days *What to do when you don't want to smile* 116

25 Trustomer Service 123

26 Are You Writing That Down? 128

27 Getting The Balance Right *Professional and friendly* 132

28 Are You Getting Too Much Recognition? 137

Say Hello 143

29 Say Hello 145

30 The Silent Language Of Listening 146

31 Social Media *The Colosseum of customer service* 151

32 Video Killed The Telephone 155

33 The Power Of Names
Personalising emotional connections 160

34 The Art Of The Greeting
One chance to make a first impression 165

35 Being Memorable: The Hook That Sticks 173

36 Don't Follow The Curve – Create it 177

37 Once Upon A... 180

38 The Power Of Positive Language 186

39 Feedback - *The gift you didn't ask for* 190

40 Mastering The Follow-Up 195

41 AI – Embrace Not Replace 199

42 How To Write So Readers Read 203

43 How To Say No Nicely 208

44 Communication In A Crisis 212

45 Learn The Language 216

46 When Less Can Be More 221

47 The Craft Of Conversation 222

48 Why Should I Use You? 227

49 Your Customer Service Brand 231

50 Build Your Bridge 235

Acknowledgements 239

About The Author 241

Other Books by Michael Heppell 242

Introduction

It was Fred who first shared those magic words with me.

Fred is a legend in the hospitality industry. You may know him as the affable maître d' in Channel 4's *First Dates,* he is...the one and only... Fred Sirieix.

I first met Fred after another behemoth of the hospitality industry, Jonathan Raggett, took me for dinner at Galvin at Windows. It was a restaurant on the 28th floor of the Hilton Hotel, Park Lane, London. 'You'll like Fred', said Jonathan with a wry grin. 'He's the spirit of 5-star service.'

And he was right. I quickly booked again, took guests and organised 'field trips' for companies who wanted to see how restaurant service should be delivered.

It was on one of these trips that Fred described the philosophy behind 'See, Smile, Say Hello'. In his deep French accent, he explained, 'Michael, hospitality is simple. Just see your customer before they see you. Smile at your customer before they smile at you. And say hello to your customer before they say hello to you.'

Could it really be that simple?

Well, yes and no.

Fred's basic principle is brilliant. It's a mantra that everyone can learn and do. But in this book, I'm taking this basic concept and, using over 25 years of teaching, presenting and writing about customer service, I'm going deeper.

See is about making every customer feel important. There are over 8 billion people on this planet. Imagine each one with a sticker on their forehead proclaiming a simple truth, 'Make me feel special'. No two people are the same and seeing individuals individually is a key to profitable customer service.

Smile is about emotional connection.

'No one cares how much you know until they know how much you care'
(This Theodore Roosevelt classic is one of my favourite quotes).

Like me, you may be guilty of wanting people to know your achievements, qualifications or expertise (I fall into that trap all the time) as it can be reassuring. But for whom? You or your customer? In most cases, I bet you would rather have a warm, caring person who may not be a technical expert, than an expert who is cold and uncaring. And before you counter with 'brain surgeon', there's increasing research that suggests patients recover faster with good 'bedside manner' so it's more than surgical skill alone. Any surgeons reading this, please can we have both?

When I was researching *See, Smile, Say Hello,* I was fortunate to meet and enjoy some conversations with Tom Kerridge. Tom is a remarkable Michelin-starred chef, restaurateur, author and TV presenter. His whole professional life has been about one thing – 'the food'.

We were discussing how the world of hospitality was changing and I asked him: 'What would you rather have – brilliant food with okay service or brilliant service with okay food?'

His answer made me more determined than ever to write this book.

If you'd like to know his response, you can watch a short video of Tom's answer on my website www.MichaelHeppell.com. The world has changed!

Say Hello is about communication. In a bonkers world where we are connected via multiple channels, devices and feeds, it's more important than ever to cut through the noise and communicate brilliantly with your customer. I'll cover language, writing, social media, good old how to talk to people and... drum roll... listen. Because as much as saying hello is important, hearing hello is equally so.

Definition Of A 'Customer'

For the simplification and benefit of your reading experience, my definition of a customer is '**anyone who isn't you**'. That means: customers in the traditional sense, those lovely people who buy your goods and services. Your teammates. Your suppliers. Your family and friends. And even (especially?) those who are serving you. Yes, EVERYONE who isn't you.

By treating everyone as a customer you'll enrich many parts of *your* life. Plus, you won't have to remember to 'turn it on' at work or in a traditional customer-facing scenario.

How To Get The Best Out Of This Book

A little bit about the mechanics of *See, Smile, Say Hello.*

There are 50 chapters. You don't have to read them all and you certainly don't have to read them in order. But I'd like you to read most of it. And I promise it's an easy read – it's written by a simple author. I've included lists, 'pop-outs' and general design ideas to make it easily digestible. You're busy, I know, so let's get to it.

The main 'pop-outs' are **Stats**, **Ripple Effect** and **'Sciencey Bits'**

Stats are research that backs up, or in some cases, challenges the idea I'm writing about. For non-fiction authors, there's a temptation to have a huge reference section at the back of a book where we quote the thousands of papers and research we've studied in the creation of our work. But there are two problems with this. One, do you ever reference them? And two, do you actually think the author has read all of them? I shared a stage with a VERY successful author (think one of the biggest non-fiction books of the decade) who confessed to me that they wrote their book then, 'Paid a post-grad student to find the references for me'. My method is a little cruder. I use 'The Google' and 'Brilliant Ai' my GPT powered assistant to help me with my research. If you'd like to know more about any of the research ask me.

The Ripple Effect was inspired by my wonderful friend Will Polston. He has a massive goal to impact 1 billion people with his work using the 'ripple effect'. In a nutshell, it means make a big positive impact with one person so they make a positive impact with 10 and so on. Customer service is the perfect way to do this. Make your customer happy and they're more likely to pass a bit of that happiness on.

Sciencey Bits are included to add the scientific research behind some of the ideas. It's ok that I think something, but who else believes it? And is there proof? This is where I used 'Brilliant Ai' which is based on my work and an added resource – all the world's documented knowledge. Of course, research and science are continually changing and evolving so I would encourage you to do your own research too.

What I'd Like You To Do

As well as my speaking, writing and business coaching, I've also helped and inspired hundreds of writers to become published authors with my 'Write That Book' programme.

New authors often say, 'If my book inspires just one person, I'll be happy.' This, of course, is rubbish. One isn't enough. Authors want armies. Thousands of people they inspired to take action and make the planet a better place because of their writing, 'Words Change Worlds'.

So, dear reader, what would be rather splendid is that if you read a chapter of this book, and you feel inspired by the idea, you then test it. Not, know it, try it or talk about it, but actually use it and see how it works. I can guarantee all of the ideas work some of the time and some of the ideas work all of the time, but only if you test them.

Think Transferable

This is the key to getting the most from this book. I've done my best to give a wide variety of examples, anecdotes and live issues. I've covered many professions, levels of responsibility and types of customers; but if your circumstance isn't mentioned, I'm sorry. I don't want to read a review that says, 'Not a mention of the Alpaca Farming Community – one star!' Just think transferable. Rather than closing the shutters because you're not in a front-line hospitality role, instead ask, 'How can I use this idea in my life now?' Do that and I think we'll get along famously.

Embrace Repetition

Almost all of the key concepts in this book will be repeated. Just as you don't learn Spanish by saying Gracias once, you don't learn the key principles of *See, Smile, Say Hello* by reading them once. I promise at some point you'll be reading a chapter and you'll have a sense of déjà vu. That's by design, to embed the principles using different tools. Sometimes a story, next time a fact, then a list or process. Each time your brilliant brain is fuelled by an idea you're more likely to use it.

The Commercial Impact

You know, I know, everyone knows, organisations that improve their customer service add profits to the bottom line. So why doesn't everyone do it?

There are many reasons and I touch on several of them in this book. The main ones are:

Don't Know

Don't Want

Don't Care

Don't Know is the easiest one to fix. Read this book, get some training, study others and pinch all their best ideas. At a time where all the world's knowledge is in your pocket, there are NO excuses.

Don't Want is trickier. It's challenging because when I talk to people (especially business leaders) they all claim to want to improve levels of service, but when I ask them what they are prepared to do, fewer can articulate it.

Christine (Mrs Heppell – you'll see her name a lot in this book) and I recently stayed in a hotel where they proudly claimed to have invested €40 million on a refurbishment. It was stunning. But after two nights we agreed the whole budget must have been spent on the building and very little on the staff. Choosing not to invest in yourself and your teams to improve levels of customer service is the same as not wanting to.

Don't Care is easier. Some organisations just don't care. In fact, some have become famous for it and argue that price is more important than service. Cheap flight to Dublin anyone? Across an organisation, nine out of ten staff may care, but one could be disillusioned, disconnected or disenfranchised. Work with the willing, ask yourself, what do YOU want to be known for and read this book for YOU.

Reading This Book

I can't dictate how you read *See, Smile, Say Hello*, you may want to start at page one and move systematically to the end reading every word on every page. Awesome!

With books like this, I'm a 'hopper'. I skim, check out the chapter headings and if I like one, dive in. But I always read with a pen. I encourage you to do the same. Make notes, scribble, add your slant and capture your thinking live. This is what will make *See, Smile, Say Hello* part of your ways of acting and doing rather than just a book you once read.

That's it. I'm ready if you're ready. Let's go!

See

1

See

In our rush to digitise and optimise, we've forgotten something. We've neglected how to see each other. Really see each other.

'See' is about reclaiming the lost art of observation. It's about looking past the transaction and recognising there's a person behind every interaction.

The customer. The colleague. The human.

By understanding your customer and treating them as an individual, it becomes easier to create a personalised service. But you have to know what to look for and what kind of personalisation is needed or even wanted.

This chapter uses See in several ways. From literally seeing your customer and the cost of what happens when you don't, to cultural observations and generational sensitivities.

2

The Personal Touch

When is a suit not a suit?

In 1846 Henry Poole opened a shop in Savile Row, London. His idea was customers would choose a cloth that was specific to their taste and their lifestyle. They would be measured and a custom-made suit would be tailored just for them. The term 'bespoke' comes from the selection of cloth, that it 'be spoken for' by individual customers. Although Henry Poole can't claim to be the inventor of bespoke tailoring, he certainly put Savile Row on the map. And he did invent the Dinner Jacket – that's a Tuxedo for my American Readers. Pretty cool eh?

A bespoke suit is a one-off in every way. If you own one, you'll know just how special you feel when you put it on.

Made to Measure uses a pattern and enables the wearer to have custom sizing and a far superior fit. I once bought a made-to-measure suit in Singapore. The tailor convinced me it would be the best suit I'd ever buy and I would have it all my life. I think it lost its shape after about six months and was in pieces shortly afterwards.

Then there's custom-made. This is where you choose from a menu of items (fabric, buttons, lapel style etc) and the trusty tailor puts it together – a one-off (ish), just for you.

What do they all have in common? The wearer feels special. And not just because of the eyewatering costs. From bespoke to customised, the whole experience makes the average wearer happy to spend the equivalent of ten to fifty times more than something off the peg at Marks & Spencer.

But still, it's just a suit.

I love it when someone remembers my name. Arriving back at a hotel after a few months (or years) and being greeted by name is the ultimate deposit in an emotional bank account. But personalisation isn't just about using someone's name. It's about understanding their preferences, anticipating their needs and crafting an experience that feels tailor-made.

This kind of attention takes effort, but it makes customers feel special and significantly boosts satisfaction, loyalty and spend.

See Stat

Research by Epsilon showed that 80% of consumers are more likely to make a purchase when brands offer personalised experiences. This isn't a gimmick; it's a strategic advantage.

Personalisation makes your customers feel valued which ultimately drives engagement and sales.

In a sea of sameness, the organisations that truly stand out are those that make their customers feel unique, seen and valued. Welcome to the age of personalisation.

Practical Steps To Personalise Your Customer's Experience

Use Data

Gather data on preferences, behaviours and past interactions. Then use this information to tailor your interactions. Be careful how you store this information as it's more important than ever to be compliant.

Segment Your Audience

Group customers by similar preferences or behaviours to target them more effectively. It's now super easy to 'tag' your customers in even the most basic database to make the way you interact with them more personal.

Tailor Your Communications

Personalise emails, messages and offers. Make each interaction feel personal and relevant.

See Stat

Research from Invesp shows there's a 29% higher open rate on emails that include a customer's name.

Offer Personalised Recommendations

Use data and algorithms to suggest products or services that match customer preferences. Not sure how? Ask The Google!

Small Data

And it's not necessarily big data that's needed. Everyone has a smartphone and on that smartphone, there's a contacts app. Every time you meet somebody take a few moments after your meeting to write a few pieces of key information in the 'notes'.

I write things like names of children, birthdays, favourite football teams etc. Then the next time I'm talking to that person I can quickly look at the notes before the conversation.

My brilliant massage therapist uses small data, She remembers lots of micro details like the client who doesn't like her feet touched, or the one who needs the blinds closed and the lights dimmed to minimum. And there's the one who talks too much and is always cold - hmm who could that be?

Small data is as powerful as big data when it comes to personalisation.

Ripple Effect

Personalisation isn't just good for customers; when employees see the impact of personalisation and how it leads to greater engagement they want to do more, go deeper and make it even more special. Customers who receive a personal service are 10x more likely to become loyal advocates, driving repeat business and referrals.

3

The Cultural Lens

In our connected world, seeing, understanding and respecting cultural differences isn't optional – it's essential. Cultural sensitivity can make or break customer interactions.

But don't fret, the good news is you don't need to be an expert on every nuance. Simply by seeing through the eyes of others, you can build stronger, more respectful relationships that enhance the customer experience and build loyalty.

Why Cultural Sensitivity Matters

Different cultures come with their specific norms, values and expectations. That includes you. In simple terms, what's considered polite in one culture might be rude in another. Being culturally sensitive means adjusting your interactions to these differences. This prevents misunderstandings and shows your customers that you respect and appreciate their backgrounds.

Here are a few examples of where one culture may differ from another. How many are you aware of?

Eye Contact

Polite in Western cultures: In countries like the UK, USA and Australia, maintaining eye contact is often seen as a sign of confidence, attentiveness and respect.

Rude in some Asian cultures: In South Korea, direct eye contact, especially with elders or authority figures, can be seen as confrontational or disrespectful.

Tipping

Generous gratuities are expected in the USA: Tipping is a crucial part of the service culture, with service staff often relying on tips to make up their wages.

Ill-mannered in Japan: In the beautiful land of the rising sun, tipping can be seen as an insult, implying that the service provided was not good enough and the server requires additional payment.

Handshake

Common in Western cultures: A firm handshake between sexes is often a standard greeting in many Western countries, symbolising trust and respect.

Inappropriate in some Middle Eastern cultures: In countries like Saudi Arabia or the UAE a handshake between a man and a woman might be seen as inappropriate, unless initiated by the woman.

Use Of First Names

Informal and friendly in the UK or USA: Using first names, even in business settings, is a sign of friendliness and approachability.

Too informal in Germany: Germans typically use formal titles and surnames, especially in professional settings, until a certain level of familiarity is reached.

Silence

Awkward in the UK: In some Western cultures, silence during a conversation can feel uncomfortable and is often filled quickly with small talk.

Polite in Finland: Silence is highly valued in Finland and it's often used as a sign of thoughtfulness or respect during a conversation.

Eating Etiquette

You may think leaving nothing on your plate is a sign of appreciation.

In some parts of China, clearing your plate can signal that you weren't given enough food, so it's polite to leave a little to show you're satisfied.

Gift Giving

Simple wrapping is enough: In the UK the wrapping of a gift is not overly scrutinised and it's the act of giving that counts. Thus the rise of reusable gift bags!

More Important in Japan: For the Japanese the way a gift is wrapped holds significant cultural value. Presentation is key and sloppy wrapping can be perceived as disrespectful.

Add dress codes, religious beliefs, personal space, punctuality, family hierarchy, hand gestures, haggling, numerology and owls and there's lots to consider. Yes, owls.

And the world is changing fast so there will be more, much more, to consider in the coming years.

Using a preferred pronoun is a simple way to show respect. And yet still some people argue, 'This wasn't a thing when…' But it was a thing. Research shows using 'they' and 'them' as individual descriptors was used in the 14th century, it's just become more important now. And if it's important to your customer, it should be important to you.

Here are a few simple ways to enhance your cultural appreciation and sensitivity:

Educate

It can be fun to learn about cultural backgrounds. This can be through formal training, reading and engaging with diverse communities.

Gamify

Could you turn the information I gave earlier into a quiz and maybe add a few more questions? Maybe find out why you shouldn't give an owl to someone from Nigeria.

Observe And Adapt

Pay attention to customers' reactions and adjust your approach. What works for one group or individual might not work for another.

Ask And Listen

Don't hesitate to ask respectful questions about cultural preferences. Listening can provide valuable insights. I promise you most people would rather be asked about their cultural preferences than you make assumptions.

Respect Differences

Appreciate different cultural practices and avoid presumptions based on stereotypes. You'll almost certainly get it wrong.

Ripple Effect

Cultural sensitivity doesn't just enhance customer interactions; it improves team dynamics and makes YOU better. As a culturally aware individual, there are dozens of benefits including improved communication, stronger relationships, enhanced empathy, better problem-solving ability, increased opportunities in a globalised world, improved conflict resolution, boosted self-awareness, greater adaptability, better tolerance, enhanced emotional intelligence and reduced prejudice.

See Stat

And if you'd still like a little more convincing McKinsey & Company found that diverse companies are 35% more likely to outperform their less diverse counterparts. A PwC survey showed that 76% of consumers prefer businesses that demonstrate cultural understanding.

Seeing through the eyes of others is a powerful skill. Enhancing cultural sensitivity creates meaningful and respectful relationships with your customers. This improves interactions, strengthens loyalty and drives success. Take the time to learn, observe, and adapt. Embrace diversity and remember: you're different too.

4

I Would Have Bought The Mercedes

Literally, See Me

When I first started my business and didn't have much (actually any!) money, I used to fantasise about owning a Mercedes SL500. Not the new model – the one with the square headlights. My dream was a bright red one with a cream leather interior, the kind of car that more than hinted, look at me!

I was skimming my local newspaper and noticed our local Mercedes dealership had one in stock. It was just two years old, red and screaming at me. Even though I could barely afford my weekly shop, never mind a new car, I decided to visit the dealership. Just to see one. Maybe sit in it.

The salesperson was brilliant. Instead of a standard test drive, he offered me the keys and suggested I, 'Take it home for the weekend.'

I was aware of the puppy dog sale and I assumed because of my cunning intellect I was in control. My thinking was, *What a genius move. I'll just enjoy a couple of days pretending, get this out of my system and then hand it back.*

For two glorious days, I lived my best life. Roof down, the sun shining, wind in my hair, king of the road. I strategically planned my journeys to squeeze out every single mile of the dealership's mileage limit.

I loved it, but, by Monday morning, reality hit. I couldn't afford the car, not even close. As I drove back to the dealership, my sensible side took over. I would hand it back, say thank you very much and move on with my life.

That was until I stopped at a red light. A car pulled up beside me, the driver leaned over, rolled down the passenger window and said, 'Beautiful car, mate.'

'Thanks!' I replied, with a ridiculous grin.

And just like that, I was no longer driving a borrowed car. In my head, it was mine. As I pulled into the dealership I had already decided. Whatever it takes I'll find the deposit. My credit card was burning a hole in my pocket. I'd sort out the payments later by cutting back on other things. Food – who needs food? And I'd buy the red SL500.

As I walked into the garage, ready to commit financial insanity, the showroom was deserted. Worse still, no one was interested in me. Two salespeople were deep in conversation – with each other. The receptionist seemed more interested in something under her nails and the sales manager hovered in his glass-fronted office, occasionally glancing up from his computer.

I was there for fifteen minutes. It felt like fifty. Wandering between cars, my enthusiasm slowly cooling. *Maybe this isn't such a good idea.*

Finally, I approached the receptionist. 'Hi, I'm just here to drop off the car I had over the weekend,' I mumbled as I reluctantly handed over the keys. She barely looked up.

As I drove away, in my boring old car, the adrenaline of the weekend was gone, replaced by relief. I'd dodged a financial bullet. Four days later, the original salesperson called. 'So, what did you think?' he asked casually.

I wanted to say, *If you or any of your colleagues had shown the slightest interest on Monday morning, you'd have made the sale.* But I simply said, 'It's not for me right now. Thank you.'

He thought it was my decision. He had no idea it was his.

In A World Where It's Hard To Be Seen, Be A Seer

It's getting harder to be seen. There are too many distractions. Some common ways to make us feel invisible are:

Trying to get the attention of a server when you'd like to spend more money on food or drinks.

Being ignored when you walk into a five-star hotel by a doorman who is too busy chatting to reception, before suddenly spotting you and offering to take your bags.

Blanked by retail assistants who would rather chat with each other than find out what you want and offer you help.

Joining a queue where the 'professional' is too important to recognise that you have been waiting for 30 minutes.

Struggling to find your platform at a station, clearly scanning for help, while nearby staff don't offer assistance.

Okay, you've got me. They are some of the ones that have happened to me and drive *me* nuts. But I'm sure there are plenty that drive you crazy too.

This is a positive book, so let's have a look at some solutions.

Think Like A Meerkat

Meerkats have a heads-up approach, constantly scanning the horizon. They work in packs (or mobs) looking out for threats or opportunities that will impact the rest of the community. Be more meerkat.

Avoid The Ask

It's stupidly simple: in a restaurant, noticing a customer's empty glass and offering a refill before they ask makes them feel cared for. On a train, offering help to someone struggling with luggage by stepping in proactively is memorable. On a flight, noticing a passenger looking cold and offering them a blanket *before* they have to ask shows thoughtfulness. What can you do before you're asked?

Eyes On The Entrance

Make it easier to have eye contact with every customer who enters your space. Sometimes a change in the layout of a room can make all the difference.

The Five-Second Rule

This is not about eating food off the floor. It's encouraging a policy where everyone acknowledges customers within five seconds of spotting them. It's as simple as showing customers they've been seen and are valued, even if immediate help isn't available.

Body Language

Most people can work out by observing body language how a person is feeling. You don't have to be a CIA interrogator to know when someone is lost, confused or frustrated.

See Stat

The desire to buy can decrease by 60% in 7 minutes if the customer is ignored. My Mercedes research proved that! The same can be said for online queries, call queues and that all-important time between finishing the main course and the highly profitable dessert.

5

The Power Of Pain

What problem are you actually solving?

At the core of every successful organisation is a simple truth: they exist to solve a problem. Not just any problem, but a real, pressing issue. The type that occupies far too much of their customer's bandwidth.

This chapter is about uncovering those precious pain points, asking the right questions, digging deeper and providing the ultimate solution.

Understanding Pain Points

Don't think about customer pain points as inconveniences. See them as the friction that slows everything down, the obstacles that prevent people from achieving their goals and the fiddly faffs and frustrations of daily life. Once you've identified these pain points, you've taken a major step towards service innovation and value creation.

No non-fiction book written since 2020 would be complete without a good Covid story. Here's mine.

At the end of 2019, my wife and I reviewed our year. It had been a busy one. We were away from home for 159 nights. Planning 2020, Mrs Heppell had one request, 'Can we spend more time at home in 2020?' 'Of course,' I promised.

And true to my word, we did spend, along with the entire planet, A LOT of time at home in 2020.

As well as writing books, I'm a professional speaker and coach. The speaking market disappeared overnight and I was left wondering what to do with myself. So, using my tools (no cobbler's shoes here), I asked my customers what I could do for them. It was a simple online survey with one question. *If I could teach you something valuable over the next 90 days what would you choose?*

How to Be Brilliant(er)
How to Save An Hour Every Day
How to create 5 Star Service during uncertain times

How to Be Brilliant(er) was a play on my book and keynote *How to Be Brilliant. How to Save An Hour Every Day* was, in hindsight, a ridiculous idea, as for the first time in years millions of people had been given more time than they knew what to do with – hence banana bread and the growth of the Zoom quiz. And *5 Star Service* was, let's say, during a global pandemic, niche.

Just as I was about to press send, I decided to add one more item to the list. 'How to write a book'. 24 hours later the results were in. Over 75% of people had ticked, How to write a book. Three years later, I'd coached over 1,000 people, ran six Masterclasses and written the book, appropriately titled, Write That Book *how to write, publish and sell your book.*

Once I decided I was going to teach people how to *Write That Book* I needed to find out why they hadn't. The 'pain' wasn't a lack of creativity, what to write about or even the ability to write – most new authors think they're pretty good at this! Ironically during this time, dozens of online writing schools popped up offering to show new authors how to write. And fix the pain that few writers thought they had.

These courses were great, but they didn't address the main problem. New writers still 'had a book *inside* them'. I wanted to create something that would purge the pain and help them to get their book out.

My research showed the pain was predominantly three things: lack of confidence, perceived cost and accountability.

My course was designed to give clear solutions to those major pain points. Not only did *Write That Book* keep me out of trouble for three years, but it also enabled hundreds of people, who previously thought they couldn't be a published author, to successfully write, publish and sell their books.

Here are five ways to identify pain points:

Ask And Listen

When creating a survey think carefully about your questions. It's difficult, but try not to create bias in your questions. It's an easy mistake, you skew the question to give the answer you want to hear rather than what your customer wants to say.

Surveys and feedback forms are great because they have the benefit of anonymity for the customer. Direct conversations can be good but be careful not to defend your position when asking questions. The time to answer and share your 'why' will come. Remember the purpose is to gather raw, unfiltered insights.

Study Your Stats

Dive into your data. Look for patterns in complaints, support tickets and reviews. What story are they telling? Remember your statistical data is only as good as your collection methods and prompts. If you want great results, you need great data.

Empathy Mapping

Step into your customer's shoes. What are they thinking? Feeling? Saying? Doing? Gaining this perspective is essential. I know, for most organisations, participating in roleplay is right up there with getting a poke in the eye with a sharp stick, but taking 30 minutes as a team to play out some customer scenarios is golden.

Customer Journey Mapping

I remember working with a business who did 80% of their business online and wanted to move to 100% in the coming 12 months. I asked their sales director about the last three things he'd bought from their site and how he'd found the process. Guess what? Of course, he hadn't used the site in anything other than sandbox mode! Use your product, examine the process, chart every step, find the friction points, address them and make that journey smooth.

Competitor Analysis

Learn from your competitors. What pain points are they solving? What are they overlooking? What can you do better and what insights can you borrow from them? There's no monopoly on great ideas.

Ripple Effect

When you identify and solve customer pain points, you don't just make your customers happy; you create evangelists. And these motivated missionaries want to spread the word. Are they preaching about you or your competition?

See Stat

Is it worth it? You know you've got a great product and you do a good job. Well, research by Gartner reports that 89% of companies compete mainly on customer experience. Addressing pain points is the linchpin of this strategy.

PwC found that one bad experience can drive one in three customers away… for good. Identifying and fixing pain points is crucial to retaining loyalty.

Identifying customer pain points is the foundation of five-star service. It's not sexy and it often goes unnoticed. If you're doing it well it *should* go unnoticed. Everyone can play their part from production to programming, maintenance to marketing and every role in between.

Dig deep, ask the tough questions and discover what problems you're solving. That's where the magic happens.

6

See Me

The Art Of Observation

Observation is more than just seeing. It's about understanding. It's about noticing the slight hand tremor, the furrowed brow, the way eyes dart or the fear in someone's tone. The choice of words and what's not being said. These are the details that reveal the true story.

They're the clues to what a person needs, what they're feeling and how you can connect with them on a deeper level.

Sciencey Bit

You've probably heard the embellished research that 93% of our communication is non-verbal and only 7% is conveyed through words. It's exaggerated because it only applies to communicating feelings or attitudes. But, and it's a big but, tone and visual cues still play a huge part in communication.

What To Do?

Some lucky people are naturally very good at spotting and interpreting these cues. Others, like me, need a little help. Here are five things you can do right now to help you see your customer in a deeper more meaningful way.

Be Present

Put down your phone. Look around. Notice the details. Be here. Right now. Observe the way someone's eyes light up when they talk about something they love. Detect the way their shoulders slump when they're tired or stressed. Don't react, just practise observing. See if you can do this for 17 minutes.

Active Listening

The next time you have a conversation listen, with your whole being. Don't you dare pick up that phone! Rather than just hearing the words, listen to the emotion behind them. Pick up on the pauses. Feel the sighs. Don't consider your response until you've heard everything. A pause before you answer is ok. We've become obsessed with filling every silence. A quiet moment is your friend.

Basic Body Language

You don't have to be an FBI profiler to pick up on body language. Just pay attention. Are they leaning in, eager to connect? Or are they pulling back, guarded? Shallow breathing, stressed? Or deep breathing, relaxed? Body language is a silent language that speaks volumes.

Environmental Cues

Look at the surroundings. What do they tell you about the person? Are they comfortable? Out of place? Look at your surroundings. Do they make people feel welcome? Experience your environment (physical and virtual) from the point of view of your customer. What message are you communicating? If you use a desk, what's the view from the other side?

Ask Better Questions

One of the best ways to see someone is to ask questions. And to see them clearer ask better questions. Don't settle for yes or no. Do you have a list of questions that dig a little deeper? We've all had the classic, 'Can I help you?' when browsing. You know the response off by heart, 'No thanks, just looking'. What if the salesperson asked, 'Good morning, have you been here before'. The response helps you to see if the customer is new – so you can start a helpful conversion from scratch. If they have visited before then you have a great conversation starter for the returning customer.

Here are a few ideas where you can use See Me – remember to 'think transferrable'. Just because you don't work in a certain sector it doesn't mean you can't adapt and use that technique.

Retail

Spot the customer who keeps picking up and putting down the same item. Approach them with genuine curiosity and say, 'I see you're interested in this. May I tell you more about it?'

Hospitality

Notice the guest who lingers near the reception desk but doesn't step forward. If possible, step out from behind the desk, offer a warm, welcoming smile and ask, 'Is there anything I can assist you with?'

Online Socials

See the person who leaves comments but hasn't made a purchase. Reply to all of their remarks. Thank them for being a supporter and tag them in a post. If you want to build a following, show them that you see them!

Healthcare

Beyond Symptoms: A patient's body language and tone can reveal more than their words. Notice the patient who avoids eye contact or hesitates when answering questions. They might be experiencing anxiety or a fear that they haven't openly expressed. On the flipside you may have a patient who knows a lot about their condition – they Googled it! By recognising these cues you can offer reassurance, perhaps by explaining procedures more thoroughly or simply offering a more empathetic ear.

Education

In a classroom setting, it's easy to focus on the students who raise their hands or participate frequently. But what about the quiet student who stares at their desk or avoids eye contact? Observing behaviour can help you to understand when a student might be struggling with the material or feeling overwhelmed. A gentle, private inquiry, 'How are you finding this?' can open up a dialogue where you can offer the support they need.

Corporate

In meetings, it's common for the more outspoken team members to dominate the conversation. Like education, observe the colleague who remains silent or who might be fidgeting or showing discomfort. Consider redirecting the discussion towards them with a question like, 'I'd love to hear your thoughts on this, what's your take?' Ensuring everyone feels seen and valued contributes to a more inclusive workplace.

Manufacturing

In a manufacturing or building environment, safety is of the utmost importance. Observe workers during their shifts. Are they moving cautiously? Do they seem fatigued? Subtle signs of weariness or discomfort might indicate it's time for a break or an adjustment in workload. Addressing these observations proactively can prevent accidents and show that you care about well-being, not just productivity.

Customer Support

Whether over the phone or via chat, there's much to observe in how a customer phrases their concerns. Are they USING ALL CAPS and lots of exclamation marks!!! A clue to frustration, or if you're my Mum, that she's got the caps lock stuck again. Do they pause before responding, suggesting hesitation or confusion? By picking up on these cues, you can tailor your response to be more patient, clear, or empathetic.

Ripple Effect

Seeing isn't just about retail customers. It's about everyone. See your colleagues. Understand their struggles, their victories. By observing and understanding, you create a culture of empathy and support. This ripple effect extends beyond the workplace. See someone at work and they'll see someone at home.

The art of observation is a lost skill that we desperately need to rediscover. It's about seeing the unseen, hearing the unspoken, feeling the emotion. When you master this art, you transform every interaction into something meaningful.

Keep looking. Start seeing. Feel the connection.

7

The Generation Game

In 1980 I became a teenager. I believe that makes me an 80's child. It was the best decade by far. I saw more bands, dated more girls and chalked up more firsts during those magical years than any decade before or since. The music was marvellous, the movies were magical and the fashion... horrendous.

And just as I declare the 80's was best, there are equal numbers who would fight for the 60's, 70's and 90's. But not the noughties, nothing happened in the noughties! If you're 34, that's a joke. If you were born in the noughties, *a joke* is where we used to be allowed to laugh at each other.

Each generation is different, has different values and likes to be seen differently.

Let's take a look at the key generations of our time and I'll focus on a few key areas including water use, money and of course, customer service:

Baby Boomers (born approx. 1946 - 1964) *also known as my Mum.* This generation experienced post-WWII economic growth and cultural shifts. They're often seen as hardworking and driven by stability and success.

Boomers value traditional financial stability, focusing on savings, pensions and homeownership. They're cautious with spending and typically avoid debt, though many carry mortgages into retirement.

Raised in an era before environmental concerns were mainstream, many Boomers are less focused on water conservation compared to younger generations. However, they do appreciate stable utilities.

Though less likely to adopt digital tools, Boomers do expect high-quality, consistent service and tend to be loyal to brands that deliver this.

Customer service for Boomers is about reliability and personal attention – they value being treated with respect and prefer face-to-face interactions.

Top Movie	*The Sound of Music*
Most Watched TV	*The Morecambe and Wise Show*
Food that defines them	*Shepherd's Pie*
Game or Toy	*Hoola Hoop*

Generation X (born approx. 1965 - 1980) *aka Me!*
Known for their independence and adaptability, they grew up during the rise of personal computers and the beginning of digital communication.

Gen X are shaped by economic instability and value financial independence. They often juggle mortgages, childcare and caring for elderly parents (the sandwich generation), making saving a challenge. Debt, particularly in the form of mortgages and credit cards, is a significant factor, but they're pragmatic about paying it off.

This generation is more eco-conscious, though not as focused on water conservation as younger cohorts. They've begun to adopt sustainable habits but tend to prioritise convenience over environmental considerations, balancing their needs between eco-awareness and practicality.

In terms of customer service, Gen X appreciates efficiency and expertise – they prefer direct, no nonsense solutions and dislike being kept waiting.

Top Movie	*Star Wars*
Most Watched TV	*Friends*
Food that defines them	*The Microwave Ready Meal*
Game or Toy	*Rubik's Cube*

Millennials (born approx. 1981 - 1996) – *my kids!*
They came of age during the rise of the internet and social media. They're tech-savvy, value experiences and are reshaping workplace expectations with their focus on flexibility and purpose-driven work.

Millennials are known for valuing experiences over material goods and are more open to debt, especially student loans. However, they're proactive in learning about finances, focusing on saving and investing, particularly in digital assets.

Water conservation and sustainability are high on their agenda – they actively seek out water-saving devices and companies that focus on environmental responsibility.

This generation is vocal about the need for businesses to not only provide good service but also demonstrate a commitment to sustainability and social responsibility.

Millennials expect instant, seamless customer service, often through digital platforms. They value transparency, authenticity and quick resolutions, preferring businesses that align with their ethical views.

Top Movie	*Harry Potter*
Most Watched TV	*Game of Thrones*
Food that defines them	*'Avo' Toast*
Game or Toy	*Nintendo Game Boy*

Generation Z (1997 - 2012) *aka my neighbour's kids*
Gen Z is highly cautious about money, avoiding debt as much as possible and seeking financial independence early. They're entrepreneurial, tech-savvy and prefer investing in stocks and digital currencies from a young age.

Sustainability is non-negotiable – they are the most eco-conscious generation, practising water conservation and seeking out companies that share their environmental values. Businesses that fail to align with these values often lose the Z's.

Gen Z expects fast, efficient customer service through digital channels, with a preference for self-service options, while also demanding transparency and ethical practices.

Top Movie	*Frozen*
Most Watched TV	*Stranger Things*
Food that defines them	*Sushi*
Game or Toy	*HoverBoard*

Generation Alpha (2013 - present) *aka my granddaughters.*
Alpha is growing up deeply immersed in technology, engaging with AI, virtual reality and smart devices from a young age.

Financially, they'll likely adopt digital tools such as mobile banking and cryptocurrencies early on. Sustainability will be central to their mindset, with water conservation and eco-friendly practices being key parts of their lifestyles.

They'll expect instant, seamless, and personalised customer service, favouring self-service options like apps and chatbots.

Their loyalty will gravitate towards brands prioritising environmental responsibility. For Generation Alpha, convenience, speed and ethical alignment will define excellent customer service.

Top Movie	*Encanto*
Most Watched TV	*Bluey*
Food that defines them	*Plant-based...*
Game or Toy	*Tablet-based games*

Each generation has grown and is growing up with different experiences, inputs and technologies, which shape their expectations and preferences.

In basic terms where younger generations might prioritise speed and digital solutions, older generations value personal interaction and reliability.

Seeing these differences should be part of every customer interaction.

Which generation are you? Consider how you felt when you read the movie, TV show, food or game listed at the end of your generation summary. Now you know how important it is to correct and tailor your service to each generation.

8

Seeing And Being Seen

You've heard the saying, 'The eyes are the windows to the soul.' But how often do we truly look into someone else's soul? At best we glance rather than see. And there's a world of difference between the two.

Looking is passive. Seeing is active. Looking grazes the surface; seeing creates connection. When you focus on someone's eyes, you send a powerful message: *I see you. You matter.* This seemingly simple act can transform fleeting moments into meaningful exchanges.

Looking vs Seeing

Have you ever felt judged by someone's gaze? My wife, Christine, sometimes notices people 'seeing her' – but not in a good way. It's the head-to-toe scan, the kind that feels more judgemental than friendly. Even a glance, when paired with the wrong facial expression, can speak volumes. It might say, *I've already decided who you are,* without a single word being spoken. Customers, colleagues, even strangers, they all pick up on these cues. And it's no surprise that those moments leave people feeling invisible or undervalued.

But let's flip the script. Imagine shifting your intent. Instead of looking at someone with judgement – or worse, indifference – try looking with curiosity, warmth and genuine interest. In a split second, you've gone from glancing to connecting.

The Power Of Eye Contact

Think about the last time someone looked you directly in the eye and smiled. Not a passing glance, but a moment of intentional connection. How did it make you feel? Probably valued. Maybe even trusted. Studies support this.

Sciencey Bit

Research from the *Journal of Nonverbal Behaviour* found that direct eye contact significantly increases trust, attentiveness and perceived honesty. People who make consistent eye contact are seen as more confident and approachable.

Eye contact isn't just about making others feel good – it's a tool for building trust and rapport. Whether in a meeting, a casual conversation, or even a brief interaction with a customer, looking someone in the eye says: *I'm here, and I'm listening.*

Distractions Are Everywhere

In today's world, making appropriate eye contact is more important than ever. Why? Because it's rare. We live in a sea of distractions – endless notifications, constant scrolling and screens that steal our attention. The simple act of looking up and meeting someone's eyes is now a superpower. It cuts through the noise and brings people back to the present.

Judging vs Connecting

The difference between judging and connecting is intention. Judging is looking someone up and down, assessing them with your gaze. It feels like a transaction – cold, detached, and, let's be honest, rude. Connecting, on the other hand, is about looking with compassion. It's not just about where your eyes land, but the energy behind them.

Are you approaching people with curiosity or indifference, friendliness or judgement? Your expression, whether intentional or not, makes all the difference.

See Stat 

According to research from the *American Psychological Association*, facial expressions and eye contact together form up to 55% of our total communication. That means how you look at someone – and how you look while looking – has a profound impact on how you make them feel.

Ripple Effect 

When you truly see someone, you don't just make them feel valued – you change how they see themselves. One intentional look can shift someone's mood, brighten their day and influence how they treat others. This ripple effect is powerful.

Seeing isn't just a skill; it's a choice. In a distracted, fast-paced world, deciding to see others – truly see them – is rare and transformative. Look people in the eye. Let them know you're present. You'll be amazed at the connections you build, the trust you foster and the lives you impact.

9

RADAR Thinking™

In The Real World

Average service is about dealing with problems after they have arisen. Good service is fixing problems as they appear. Brilliant service is being prepared for and having solutions to every eventuality before it happens.

RADAR Thinking™ became one the most popular tools from my book *5 Star Service* and a favourite 'Sizzle Session' in our *Hearts and Minds* training programmes.

Thousands of organisations have used it to anticipate needs and deliver proactive solutions before they're even requested. RADAR is a simple acronym.

Realise
Assess
Decide
Act
Review

By anticipating needs and addressing potential issues before they arise, you can prevent dissatisfaction and build stronger, more loyal customer relationships.

Simple. Yes, but it takes some effort.

Mack was a coaching client who owned a gym. I'm sure you know that gyms make their money from our 'best intentions'. Mack was bemoaning the fact that there had been a plethora of money advice gurus suggesting that, 'A great way to save money is to cancel your gym membership'. Unfortunately for Mack, this message appeared to be getting through and impacting his business. When I first met with him, he was losing members like lemmings off a cliff.

Using RADAR Thinking™ it took just three short turbo coaching sessions to create a plan to reduce those leaving his gym and boost his membership.

Here are my notes from our sessions.

Problem: Losing Gym Members

Clients are cancelling their memberships, class attendance is dwindling and even regulars seem to be vanishing. If you're not careful, this trickle could turn into a flood.

Step 1: Realise

Clients aren't visiting as often. Membership cancellations are creeping up. Easy to blame Martin 'Money Saving Expert' Lewis. But what was really going on?

Are members feeling like the gym no longer meets their needs? Have you been running the same classes for too long? Are your facilities showing their age? Maybe members aren't getting the personal attention they crave.

Collect data. Quick survey. Informal interviews. Ask members who have left for feedback.

This isn't about guessing; it's about **Realising** the root cause.

Step 2: Assess The Situation

The following week he had information. Time to **Assess**.

The gym wasn't losing members because of a new competitor or finances. Members felt unmotivated and disconnected. Some said they'd outgrown the classes and others felt they weren't making progress. A couple felt ignored by the staff and several (including some men) felt it was too male-oriented.

Making sense of the feedback was a revelation. Only one person said it was because they could no longer afford it. The **Assess** element helped Mack to find patterns and understand what was genuinely driving people away. But the biggest breakthrough came when he realised that 80% of leavers hadn't visited for at least 8 weeks before they quit.

RADAR is more than firefighting symptoms; it's getting to the heart of the problem.

Step 3: Decide

Now comes the tricky part – deciding what to do. The beauty of RADAR Thinking™ is it keeps you from making hasty decisions. Instead of trying to overhaul everything, the secret is to focus on targeted actions that will have the greatest impact.

Here's what he decided to do. Offer three new dynamic classes and introduce mindfulness sessions. Launch a 'Keep a Customer' campaign and invest in some staff training sessions (they hadn't had any formal training since the gym opened!).

The key was to focus on the changes that would most effectively address the core issues.

Don't try to do everything at once; **Decide** on the actions that will have the greatest positive effect and test those first.

Step 4: Act

The three new classes were launched. Two worked, and one didn't. The Mindfulness Sessions became an instant hit and they were expanded to Eat, Sleep and Stretch sessions.

Staff were incentivised to **Act** and engage with anyone who hadn't visited the gym for 4 weeks. If a team member could encourage a lapsed member to visit in the next 7 days, they got a small bonus. The team quickly discovered many members just needed a nudge. Text messaging was as successful and sometimes more effective than calls; so they automated the system to check in with members, follow up after a 4-week 'no show' and invite them back with a tempting offer.

They also stepped up their social media posts with a content-only, NO SELLING – 90-day campaign. By tagging members, sharing success stories and giving free advice they became the go-to page for health and fitness advice.

Step 5: Review

The final part of RADAR Thinking™ is to **Review**. This isn't a 'set it and forget it' process. You need to track the results and be willing to adjust if things aren't working as expected.

After 90 days Mack reviewed what had worked, what hadn't and the impacts made. The most effective part of the plan was 'Keep a Customer' the least effective were the new classes. In the end, they kept one out of the three. The additional wellness sessions became a USP and during lockdown, when many other gyms closed, he switched these sessions online and retained his members. And the best bit was that Mack got his mojo back.

See Stat

A study by Forrester Research found that proactive customer service can reduce customer complaints by up to 25%.

Why RADAR Thinking™ Works

The beauty of RADAR Thinking™ is that it helps you stay proactive rather than reactive.

Losing members from your gym or being the 2nd best rated joiner in town, doesn't have to feel like a crisis. With RADAR, you can **Realise** a problem early, **Assess** it properly, **Decide** on what's best, **Act** decisively and **Review** to ensure success.

10

The Devil Is In The Detail

It started with a recommendation. 'Michael, you and Christine must go to this restaurant. You'll love it.' Our friend was so effusive about this place that we made a booking.

Three weeks later my heart sank. On arrival, it was clear: beyond pretentious. I adore fine dining and can hold my own in most settings, but this was the kind of restaurant where the staff seemed to think they were the stars. The explanation of each dish took longer than eating it. And the bill? Eye-watering.

Their pièce de resistance was a show kitchen, one of those places where guests were expected to bow at the altar of the wannabe celebrity chef.

Yet, the details – ah, the details – betrayed them. Mistakes with the order, dingy toilets and by 8 pm, no toilet paper in the ladies' loo. Unbelievable. When we left at 10:30pm it was still the same.

The point? Don't put yourself out there as world-class if you can't get the basics right.

Retail Is Detail: Why It Matters

It's the small things that can make the biggest difference. In hospitality, a smudge on a glass, a missing napkin or a fake smile can overshadow an otherwise stellar experience. Customers remember how you made them feel and the devil is always in the detail.

In retail, a window display can make the difference between walking in or walking past.

Online, a simple message can make the difference between clicking through or carrying on browsing.

In transport, cleanliness, clear signage and real-time information can transform a frustrating journey into a smooth one. A driver helping with luggage leaves a lasting impression.

If a guest changes something in their room, leave it! Better still, if they return, recreate it.

If you want to see an extraordinary example of where detail can make a difference, just take a look at some property listings. Some sellers take the time to stage their homes leaving you thinking you must book a viewing. Others think nothing of leaving piles of laundry, badly made beds and even dirty dishes in the photographs.

See Stat 

Research from the *Journal of Customer Psychology* found that first impressions are formed within seven seconds. If those seconds reveal cracks, dirty menus, inattentive staff, out-of-stock basics, etc. you're already climbing an uphill battle to recover.

Some Practical Steps To Nail The Details

Obsess Over Basics

Spotless spaces, clear signage and well stocked essentials. These aren't optional; they're foundational.

Anticipate Needs

Offer before being asked is a fundamental of *See, Smile, Say Hello.* Proactive service beats reactive every time. If you notice a customer's glass is low or they're glancing around for help, then jump in before they ask.

Ask For Feedback

Don't wait for a TripAdvisor tirade. Proactively ask customers, 'How are we doing?' and act on what they share.

Know What Makes It/You Special

I've found myself happily paying double the price I normally would for a loaf of bread, because the staff at the bakery love to share the details. The 'ancient grains' the 'special proving methods' and 'low GI' make it even more delicious and healthy!

Make It Personal

A handwritten 'thank you,' remembering a name or offering a tailored suggestion turns an okay experience into a memorable one.

Ripple Effect

A small act of attentiveness can brighten someone's day, prompting them to pass that positivity on to others. Imagine how commuter's moods are lifted by a clean, well-maintained train. Detail has the power to affect communities, shape perceptions and even elevate industries. By setting the standard, you inspire others – competitors, collaborators and customers alike – to aim higher and care more.

F Off Fine

Customers rarely rave about 'fine.' They champion the extraordinary. And often, the extraordinary isn't in grand gestures but in nailing the tiny details. Get the basics right and everything else follows.

11

Convenient For Whom?

Why I'm not a fan of the scan

Software trainer Oz du Soleil (cool name) walked out of his brunch before he'd even ordered his mocha latte. And it was for a very specific reason. He wasn't ignored, it wasn't anything to do with fellow diners or even the price. It was because he was required to use a QR code to order from a digital menu.

The QR (Quick Response) Code is one of those peculiar ideas which was developed for a very specific reason but became popular for much more.

They were invented in 1994 by Masahiro Hara when the limitations of the barcode made it difficult to track parts in the automotive industry. He came up with the idea while he was playing the grid board game 'Go'. Clever bloke. By 2000 there was an international standard and in 2002 the first mobile phones that could read QR codes were being produced.

See Stat

Barcodes can produce up to 1 trillion possible combinations. That's a 1 followed by 11 zeros. The potential combination of QR codes is 1 followed by... 9,423 zeros!

QR codes slowly grew in popularity with the general public, then in 2020 with the Pandemic (and nobody wanting to touch menus), restaurants created QR code versions. There was a certain novelty in scanning the code and reading the menu on your phone, but like any novelty, it's worn off.

However, too many restaurants seem to be run by the finance department. Even though we are now allowed to touch paper, there still seems to be a plethora of places where you're expected to use your phone to peruse what's on offer. And here's where the accountants have got it wrong.

Diners order less (around 10 – 15%) when using QR code menus than traditional printed ones.

When you take a moment to consider, it makes perfect sense. With paper menus, you can see all of the choices rather than having to scroll or open separate sub-menus. Diners don't like friction, so when it comes to placing an order it's easier to just pick one thing and move on rather than adding sides and starters.

And when it comes to desserts, often the most profitable part of the meal, having to use your phone to scan the QR code again, then find something which you probably shouldn't be eating anyway, is a surefire way to prevent your customers from ordering anything more.

You can probably tell I'm not a fan of the scan.

Is this because I'm an old fart? No! Younger people, good old Gen Z, are even less likely to want to use QR codes than me and Millennials want personal service more than any of us.

Some chapters don't need any further explanation so let's wrap this up. When creating something which is considered 'convenient', ask yourself 'Who is this convenient for?

If it's just for you, you may enjoy a short-term profit boost but in the long-term, your savvy customers will let you know that they have options.

If it's for your customer it's worthwhile considering the cost and deciding if it's something you need to do and can afford to do.

And if it's genuinely more convenient for everyone, what's stopping you?

12

Never Knowingly Underwhelmed

There's a famous department store in the UK which is special because it's a partnership – all of the staff own all of the shops. I can't tell you how much it troubles me to write this chapter, as this once famous store that was *never knowingly undersold,* has become, for me, often knowingly underwhelming.

I can only talk for my local branch, but what used to be a guaranteed pleasant shopping experience has, over the last few year, only become a necessity. Ridiculously and with an open heart and wallet, I find myself giving them one more, ultimate, last, final, chance.

Remember the basic principle of this section of the book? See me. You would think in a retail environment this could and should be easy. Especially in a modern store with vast open spaces and fewer in-store customers than ever.

Unfortunately, what seems to happen is retail *assistants* have become one of three personas:

'The Glance'

This is my collective noun for a group of retail workers who would rather chat with each other than help customers. You can find them, usually in twos, or threes, having a good old natter about anything other than work. They catch you out of the corner of their eye (the glance) but the conversation is far too good to stop talking and start serving.

The Inst-Assistant

Those having a sneaky look at their phone, rather than looking at and seeing their customer before we see you.

The Don't-Buy-Stander

This is where the self-doubters lurk. Perhaps it's a training issue or maybe they've tried, 'Can I help you', and heard 'No thanks, I'm just looking', so many times it's dragged them down. They've just stopped connecting.

In a world where the retailer's competition is a smartphone, tablet or laptop, next-day delivery and free returns, can you imagine the impact you could make by actually connecting with customers?

And if I worked for a store where I was given a percentage of the profits as a partner, I know what I would be doing. But that's just me. What about you?

Remember when reading this, if you're thinking it's a relief that you don't work in retail; wake up – you do. Think transferrable, how do these ideas impact your work?

Why Do You Shop?

There was a time when going to the shops was a fun thing to do and if you were fortunate enough to have a little bit of cash in your pocket, that experience could be magnified. Money is the ultimate magnifier.

Now that physical shopping has become a necessity rather than a treat (and most customers aren't experiencing amazing levels of service), if you're a retailer, or work in a retail environment, you should be clicking your heels reading this.

Just train your staff to provide better experiences than the ones I've just described and you'll clean up.

Here's how:

Be A Spotter

The first and most important task is to make eye contact with everyone as they arrive or walk through your department. Give a genuine smile and say 'hello'. Sound familiar?

Do that and you're already smashing the competition.

Stop The Goss

Stop chatting to your colleagues – unless it's essential. If you put as much effort into talking to customers as many so-called retailers do talking to each other, you can't fail to sell more.

Be Interested Over Interesting

You could be a terrible salesperson and still outsell everyone by simply showing interest and talking to more people than your competition.

Practise Your Patter

Remember, your customers are programmed to say, 'No thank you, I'm just looking', especially if you ask the age-old, and thoroughly boring question, 'Can I help you?

Even if your customer **does** need help, their auto-response is set to, 'No thanks, I'm just looking'. So how about having a few opening lines that are designed to engage customers?

'Have you been here before?'

'That's new stock, it's just arrived.'

'Have you seen the X version of that? It's beautiful.'

'Lots of people have been looking at Y today.'

'What brings you in today?'

'I saw you looking at A, can I show you B? I think you might like it. '

'Can I offer some advice on this?'

'Have you seen the special offer we have on Z at the moment?'

Even, 'I'm here if you need anything, but take your time.' Is better than nothing.

See Stat

Research by *RetailNext* showed that conversion rates increase by 15% just by creating engagement with browsing customers.

And on the flip side, research by *Zendesk* showed that 40% of customers who need help, but can't immediately find it, abandon their purchase.

Considering the decline of the high street, the fact that millions of people still take the time to walk into a store, means they want to buy something. And if they don't buy from you they will find it somewhere else.

Your job is to engage, put deposits in your browser's emotional bank accounts and make sure the buying process is as simple and seamless as possible.

13

Sell Me More

Upselling with integrity

Christine and I hired a motorhome and drove to Brighton for a weekend music festival. The motorhome was described as a two-berth. I think the two berths were built for Sneezy and Bashful. The site had beautiful views but there was no power and one water tap supplied all the motorhome users. Let's just say that by the end of the weekend, we were ready for home, a hot shower and a comfortable bed.

The following year I ASKED, the motorhome rental company if they had anything bigger or better than the Snow White Special. Guess what? They did. Christine loved it, did most of the driving and quickly became known as the Mother Trucker.

That year, when we arrived on the site, we noticed one line of motorhomes had electric hook-up points. When we asked the organisers if we could have one they explained that they didn't think there would be much demand as it was an expensive option (£45 for the weekend) so they'd only offered it to a few customers.

The following year over half the motorhomes had paid for an electric hook-up, there were more taps than people and our home on wheels was a monster!

The festival was better, our comfort was greater and our overall experience was enhanced.

And yes we'd paid more – with joy!

The main reasons why upselling is often seen as a dodgy activity is because the upsell isn't valued or the seller doesn't believe in what they are selling.

In customer service, recognising and executing potential opportunities to upsell is crucial. Upselling isn't about pushing more expensive products or services for the sake of it; it's about offering solutions that genuinely meet your customer's needs. Your customers will do more to avoid pain than gain pleasure.

Let's explore how to identify upsell opportunities, build more confidence to suggest them, execute upsells effectively and sell with integrity.

Why Upselling With Integrity Matters

Upselling with integrity means offering a product or service that genuinely adds value for your customer. I believe, when done correctly, upselling enhances the customer experience, builds trust and increases satisfaction.

Most customers appreciate recommendations that solve their problems more effectively, even if it means spending a little (or sometimes a lot) more to achieve it.

See Stat

Research by the Journal of Business Research shows that upselling can increase revenue by up to 30% when executed correctly. Customers are 70% more likely to purchase an upsell when they perceive it as a beneficial recommendation rather than a sales tactic.

One of our favourite clients own a selection of four and five-star hotels. Recently we were working with their London teams. During a conversation with their Director of People, we discovered that a primary reason they missed opportunities to upsell a larger room, offer a more luxurious wine, suggest an experience, entice a dessert, or a dozen other enhancements, was the belief that the customer wouldn't want to *pay more* for the product or experience. With this mindset, the idea of suggesting anything from a glass of champagne to a park view suite was often missed.

The irony is that most guests are paying over £500 a night to stay in these hotels. Welcome to London.

In most cases, it's down to confidence. But the idea of just *being more confident* is ridiculous. Confidence isn't something you have it's something you do. And it's easier to 'do confident' when it's built on a tool or technique.

Here are three tools we shared that can be learned by anyone:

Go For No

This is a classic *Flip It* technique. When you're yearning for a yes, it can feel awkward and maybe come over as a little desperate. When your expectation is 'no' it's possible to ask an upsell question multiple times and consider every 'no' as a win. Even if you receive ten 'no's' to every 'yes' – you still win.

Act As If

Having a conversation acting *as if* your customer always wants the upsell is a great default position. My hairdresser Richard is hopeless at upselling. He NEVER asks me if I would like to buy a product. When I challenged him on this he shared that he assumed I would say 'no'. I asked if maybe he didn't believe in the products. He then spent the next ten minutes telling me how brilliant they were, how he'd visited the factory in Italy, why they were great value as you needed less because the quality was so good. But he still didn't ask me if I wanted a tin of the wax he applies after every cut.

He's still acting *as if*. Acting as if no one will buy a product!

But what if he acted as if EVERY customer wanted just one product and added *Go For No*? What if he offered a shampoo, conditioner, wax or gel to every client? Let's say seven out of eight daily customers say 'no'. That's only one sale per day. But that sale makes £6 profit. He works 170 days a year which means just over £1,000 a year will drop to the bottom line.

Ripple Effect

Richard and his wife employ 10 staff at their salon. They all watch the principals and follow what they do. 10X the asks10X the profit.

Ask Jeff

Ask yourself what would you do if the richest retailer in the world were your customer. Would you flinch asking Jeff Bezos if he wanted the best room? Jeff may have started Amazon on a desk made of a door perched on two A-frames, but now he likes the best. Have you seen his yacht?

These tools are a fun and practical way to practise upselling, but they only work if they are built on the *Seven Steps of Upselling With Integrity*. You can buy these seven steps as an additional download here....

Only kidding, lesson one

Identify Genuine Opportunities

Don't Upsell Something That You Would Normally Include For Free

Look for opportunities where an upsell truly adds value. For example, a higher-end product with better features, a service package that offers more comprehensive coverage, or an accessory that enhances the primary purchase.

Understand Customer Needs

Listen carefully to your customers to understand their needs and preferences. Ask open-ended questions to gather detailed information about their requirements.

Educate Your Customers

Provide clear and honest information about the benefits of the upsell. Help customers understand why the additional investment is worthwhile and how it addresses their specific needs.

Do Confident

Train your team to be confident in their recommendations. Role-playing exercises, success stories and positive reinforcement can help build this confidence. Remember, confidence comes from knowing your product and believing in its value.

Use A Consultative Approach

Approach the upsell as a consultant rather than a salesperson. Focus on solving the customer's problem or enhancing their experience rather than just making a sale.

Handle Objections Gracefully

Be prepared for objections and handle them with empathy and understanding. Address concerns honestly and provide additional information to reassure the customer.

Some Will, Some Won't, So What?

Remember this mantra.

It's tough to have a bad day if you did your best, gave it your all and still no one bought. But it's a disaster compared to having a bad day just because you didn't ask.

The goal is to make recommendations and offers that genuinely benefit your customers. Do this and, rather than a sales tactic, you'll turn upselling into a service.

Smile

14

Smile

A smile isn't just a gesture. It's a signal.

It says, 'I'm happy to see you.'

It says, 'You matter.'

This section is based on the premise that if you create a deeper emotional connection with your customers you'll build trust, you'll receive fewer complaints and your customers will be happy to spend more with you.

But there's something else. Your customers will benefit enormously and but you'll also reap incredible rewards for yourself. You must have been hiding under a rock for the last 20 years if you haven't seen the evidence that suggests your physical health is directly related to your emotional health. As you read these chapters, I'd like you to keep in mind that the most important person in the world is still you. Building a strong emotional connection with yourself is as important as building a strong emotional connection with others.

Remember in the introduction when I shared the story of how Fred Sirieix introduced me to See, Smile, Say Hello? The concept of smiling at your customers before they smile at you sounds simple.

But what if you don't want to smile? What if you're having a bad day? What if your customers don't deserve a smile?

This is where your internal dialogue, connections, switches, memories, beliefs and values come into play. And why I think this section of the book is as important for personal development as it is for customer service.

15

The Science Of Smiling

Creating emotional connections

A smile is more than a facial expression; it's a gateway to building emotional connections.

I love a bit of sciencey stuff. In this chapter, you're going to explore the science of smiling, its evolutionary roots and its role in bridging gaps and forging relationships. And you'll also discover why Thailand is known as the Land of Smiles.

Why We Smile

Smiling is a universal behaviour that's deeply embedded in our evolution. It signals friendliness, trust and approachability. From an evolutionary perspective, it's believed smiling developed to communicate non-threats and build social bonds. It has become a fundamental part of human interaction.

Sciencey Bit 

Research from UC Berkeley reveals that smiling activates the brain's reward mechanisms more effectively than chocolate. When you smile, your brain releases endorphins – natural painkillers – and serotonin. That makes you feel good. Very good.

And the best bit? It works both ways, benefitting both the person smiling and those on the receiving end.

My friend Matt, who typeset this book, lives in Thailand. Whenever I do a live event online, Matt tunes in and writes in the comments, 'Hi, it's Matt from the Land of Smiles'.

Thailand is famously known as the Land of Smiles. This cultural emphasis on smiling reflects their societal value of harmony and friendliness.

The Thai language has multiple words for different types of smiles:

- Yim thak thaai: A polite smile given to strangers.
- Yim cheun chom: A smile of admiration.
- Fuen Yim: A forced smile, often used in awkward situations.
- Yim tak taan: A business smile for formal settings.
- Yim mee lay: A mischievous smile.
- Yim tang nam dtah: A sincere, joyful smile that reaches the eyes.
- Yim yoh-yor: A teasing smile.
- Yim sao: A sad smile, reflecting resilience.
- Yim mai ork: A smile that hides true feelings, masking discomfort.

And in English, we have maybe one or two descriptors, such as grin, smirk or beam. It's no wonder Thailand is more impactful with smiles. They have a better 'smile toolbox'.

When I present a *See, Smile, Say Hello* Keynote or training I love to play a game with the audience called Pass The Smile.

It's simple but has a profound effect.

I begin by asking the audience how important they believe smiling is. Of course, this gets a universal thumbs-up. But then I ask, 'If it's so important, how much time do you practise smiling?' This gets a universal thumbs-down. Then I'll ask, 'If smiling is so important, why don't we practise? And then I challenge the audience; it's because we've never had to consciously practise smiling. That is, until now...

To the background of 'I love your smile' by Shanice, I challenge the audience to create and then share with three different people the following smiles.

The first is a simple 'happy to see you', where I ask the audience to imagine meeting someone who they deeply love, but who they haven't seen in a long time.

The second is a 'sneaky smile', the 'I know something you don't know' smile.

Next, it's the smile of a 'six-year-old on Christmas morning'. That moment when they walk into the lounge and discover, 'He's been!'

This is followed by the 'inner confidence smile'. Being happy with yourself and feeling good in your own skin.

And finally, I challenge the audience to show and share their best 'sexy smile'. There's much laughter.

This whole exercise takes approximately two minutes and, although it's a lot of fun, there's a serious point too. After the exercise I ask how the room feels after just two minutes of smiling.

The answer is always positive. Smiling looks good and feels good. Even thinking about smiling releases those magic endorphins.

So what's stopping you? This is where gamifying is a brilliant idea. Remember what Fred said? You must smile at your customer *before* they smile at you. That's the game, it's what makes it fun.

But often we need to be reminded. My wife will often ask, 'Are you happy?'

'Yes,' I reply.

'Well tell your face,' is her hilarious response.

It's great that I have a partner who will prod me, especially while we are setting up for events. A lot is going on and it's easy for me to forget.

Visual reminders to smile can make a difference too.

Back office areas could have a big smile poster on the door, making it the last thing team members see before heading into a public area. You can make catching each other smiling a fun activity and award prizes for the *Smile Of The Week*. Why not give out stickers. Everyone loves a sticker!

Ripple Effect

If there was ever a perfect example of the ripple effect in action it would be smiling. It improves individual interactions and fosters a positive culture. Employees who feel connected and valued are more likely to excel. For customers, a business exuding warmth and friendliness earns loyalty too.

Understand Cultural Contexts

Although I'm a raving fan of a smile, remember various cultures perceive smiling differently. For some, excessive smiling can seem insincere; in others, it's a sign of warmth. Use your gut. Smiling more is brilliant most of the time. But there's a time and a place, see Chapter 3 – The Cultural Lens.

Sciencey Bit

UC Berkeley research shows smiling activates brain reward mechanisms more effectively than chocolate. Combine eating chocolate and smiling – mmmm.

16

Confidence vs Arrogance

Confidence. Arrogance. Two words that sometimes appear dangerously close, yet in practise they couldn't be further apart. They sit on the same spectrum, but I believe there's a magic ingredient that puts them at opposite ends.

The difference between confidence and arrogance isn't about how loudly you speak, how you dress, how much you know or even how others perceive you.

It boils down to one simple factor: **Intent.**

Confidence comes from a place of wanting to help others. You're confident when you believe in yourself and the goal is outward – to lift others, inspire or offer solutions. When you're confident, you use your strength to bring value to those around you. You make people feel safe, comfortable and motivated.

Arrogance, on the other hand, is self-serving. It's often about trying to prove you're the smartest, the best or the most important person in the room. An arrogant person is focused on their image and achievements (often exaggerated). Sometimes using their knowledge or abilities to put others down. Instead of helping, their intent might be to elevate themselves at the expense of others. Dare I say 'narcissist'?

The Power Of Inner Confidence

Inner confidence radiates in the way you smile, speak and even carry yourself. It doesn't shout; it's a quiet, calm assurance that you are capable, that you can navigate challenges and that you're here to contribute something valuable. Inner confidence draws people toward you because they can sense you're genuine.

Think about the last time you were helped by someone who was confident in their role.

When Confidence Is King

I'm one of those painful people who, when asked what I'd like in a cocktail bar, flips it and asks the bartender what they enjoy making. I know from the response whether I'm going to enjoy the next few minutes. If I hear something like, 'What do you like?' or 'What would you normally have?' I know the bartender probably wasn't listening, isn't interested, lacks confidence or all three.

But if I hear, 'Do you prefer whisky or gin?' and followed up with, 'Got it, you're going to love this,' the chances are I'll be all smiles and silliness for the next five minutes. If not, I only have myself to blame because I initiated the conversation.

However, there is an important caveat, and that is they must be doing it for my benefit and not theirs. There's a thin line between being a cocky cocktail maker and a majestic mixologist.

When Arrogance Creeps In – And How We Miss It

Sometimes, arrogance sneaks up without us even realising it. We all have moments where we cross the line from confidence into arrogance and we're the last to realise.

While confidence lifts, arrogance alienates. The key difference is that arrogance is rooted in the desire to prove you're better than others.

The Humble Brag

Social media is the ultimate magnifier for this. I follow a whole range of experts, teachers, coaches and fascinating freaks who, even though I know I should, I just can't unfollow.

There's one who loves sharing pictures that take the humble brag to the next level. Strategically placed designer labels, 'Just a little update to my followers from the back of a yacht' and whoops, I accidentally seem to have caught my perfectly placed Birkin bag in that picture.

Part of me thinks good for you, but there's a bigger part that makes me wonder what she's looking for. It's not money, she's making lots of it, or at least she tells her followers she is. It's something else. I hope she finds it.

And it's not just in business. You see this in many different areas. Here are a couple of examples.

Academia (Scientists Or Professors)

Confidence: In an academic setting, a confident scientist or professor engages with colleagues and students with an open mind. Arrogance means dismissing alternative viewpoints, refusing to admit when they don't know something and belittling students or colleagues who challenge them.

Confident professors present their research with pride, but also acknowledge the contributions of others and remain open to questions and challenges. Their goal is to advance knowledge, not to prove that they're right. And because they inspire trust and collaboration, their students or peers are more likely to engage positively with them and they produce even better work.

Arrogant academics might present their work as beyond criticism. This not only stifles conversation but can also alienate those around them, making others less likely to collaborate or feel valued.

Doctors

It's an old joke, but let's do it anyway. What's the difference between a doctor and God? God doesn't think he's a doctor.

In healthcare, the difference between a confident and an arrogant doctor can be life changing and lifesaving. A confident doctor listens carefully, explains options clearly and most importantly involves the patient in their care decisions. They acknowledge when they don't know something and collaborate with others to find the best solution.

An arrogant doctor, on the other hand, might dismiss a patient's concerns, interrupt them mid-sentence or act as if their knowledge is beyond question. This can leave patients feeling ignored, anxious and ironically less likely to follow medical advice.

A confident doctor focuses on what's best for the patient. An arrogant doctor focuses on proving they're the expert.

Tech Experts Or Engineers

In a high-stakes tech environment, perhaps when a company's system goes down, a confident IT professional stays calm, assesses the problem and communicates regularly with the team.

An arrogant IT specialist might handle the same situation by keeping information to themselves, condescendingly over-explaining technical details and acting as if the rest of the team aren't capable of understanding.

Confident specialists aim to resolve the issue as quickly as possible and with their calm confidence keep everyone focused on a solution.

Arrogant authoritarians make the situation worse. Instead of building trust they alienate the team, making others feel less competent or excluded from the solution.

Every business, every role and every service has examples at both ends of the spectrum.

How To Spot The Difference

How do you know when you've tipped into arrogance? Brace yourself... Other people will spot it long before you do. Eeek! Pay attention to the non-verbal feedback you get in human interactions. Do people start backing off, giving fewer responses or nodding without engaging? That's a sign they may feel overpowered by you. When your words don't encourage conversation but instead shut it down, you might be crossing that line.

One way to check yourself is to ask: who is benefiting from this?

If you're genuinely confident, you'll see how your actions are helping others. If you're starting to feel the need to impress or show off, that's a red flag that arrogance may be creeping in.

Ripple Effect

> Confident people love to see others doing well. They'll share their ideas and feel successful when they see other people being successful. This is a true demonstration of The Ripple Effect. 'The higher tide means all ships rise' is the perfect analogy.

Let's finish on a high.

Why Confidence Leads To Brilliance

Being confident doesn't mean being perfect. Being confident doesn't mean you won't make mistakes. Real confidence is knowing you *can* make mistakes and still move forward. That's the brilliance of it – confidence encourages a growth mindset. You're always learning, adapting and willing to hear feedback because you know it helps you improve.

And if you need one more reason to drop the arrogance... Arrogance is fragile. It resists feedback because it's built on the egotistical illusion that you're already perfect. It's defensive and often crumbles under pressure.

It all leads back to intent.

When you're confident, your actions are for others.

When you're arrogant, your actions are for yourself.

This is a customer *service* book. It's the quiet humility behind service confidence that makes it powerful and lasting. While arrogance, no matter how well disguised, is often damaging and always remembered by those on the receiving end.

Have confidence in your smile. Walk into every situation with the intention of helping. Aim to contribute and to lift others. That's real confidence.

Your customers will notice and they'll love you for it.

17

Trusting Your Gut

How to harness emotional intelligence

Emotional Intelligence (EI or EQ – depending on the day of the week) is a game-changer in customer service.

When I first read about EQ, the focus was very much around understanding your emotional intelligence. This developed into managers wanting to understand their teams and have their teams understand them. Many surveys and diagnostics were created and rolled out so staff could be given a 'profile', describe themselves as a 'Purple Thruster Monkey' and forever justify why they didn't have to wash a mug or stick to a budget. 'It's not my fault, it's my personality type'.

Now, amongst the bollocks, there's a realisation that, guess what, it's not all about you. Understanding your own emotions is great, but sensing and responding to the emotions of others and your customers is a game changer.

Emotional Intelligence means perceiving, understanding and managing emotions. That's the intelligent bit. In customer service, it's about reading between the lines, sensing unspoken needs and responding in a way that makes customers feel understood and valued.

Here's how:

Start With Yourself

I know it can be a bit of a pain having to contemplate oneself first, especially for us Purple Thruster Monkeys, but understanding your emotions and how they affect your interactions is key. You may not be the only person who is triggered by noisy eaters or people who don't say please or thank you. Reflect on your triggers and practise some exploratory self-talk to help your understanding that it is just a feeling, to stay present and know that it will pass.

Cultivate Empathy

Put yourself in the customer's shoes (sorry about the cliché). Listen actively and do your best to understand their feelings. Using a phrase like 'I understand how you feel' to show empathy is good, genuinely saying it and knowing how a person might feel is very powerful.

Trust Your Gut

Trust your intuition about what your customer needs. If you sense frustration, offer a solution before they voice it. Your intuition is normally accurate.

Practice Active Listening

Do what it takes to pay full attention to your customer. Easier said than done, see Chapter 30. Summarise what they've said to ensure understanding and to show that you're listening.

Manage Your Emotions

Yep, back to you. It's always about you. Stay calm and composed, even in challenging situations. Practise techniques like deep breathing when you don't need it, to maintain control when you do.

Develop Your Social Skills

Building rapport through quality small talk and taking a genuine interest in your customer's well-being is a skill. Some people make it look effortless, for others it can be cringing.

Have you watched the TV show *First Dates?* The awkwardness of some poor bloke (and it's normally the bloke) not knowing what to say, what question to ask or how to give a compliment, leaves you feeling drained. And that's just for the viewer.

Social interaction is something that can be practised. In my book *How to Be Brilliant*, as part of the challenge to build confidence, I ask readers to start five conversations with five strangers. For some this is a huge ask and for others it's easy. How would you feel?

Smile Stat

TalentSmart's research shows on average, people with high 'EI' Emotional Intelligence, annually earn £20,000 more than those with low EI.

Trusting your gut and harnessing emotional intelligence can transform ordinary interactions into extraordinary experiences. It's not just about what you do, but how you make people feel that creates lasting impressions. I'm challenging you to use your emotional intelligence to connect, empathise and deliver exceptional service. Even you Purple Thruster Monkeys.

18

Malaga Eggs

If the customer doesn't see it, does it matter? Small fibs don't really hurt anyone. As long as the end result looks okay, there's no real harm done. Yes, some people subscribe to this because they think they'll be the ones who won't get caught.

Customers notice more than you think.

When you find a business cutting corners, lying, or being dishonest, you don't just feel let down at that moment. It damages trust forever. And once trust is broken, it's almost impossible to rebuild.

We were staying in the beautiful city of Malaga. It was our first morning in a charming city hotel and Christine ordered scrambled eggs for her breakfast. Simple. Nothing complicated.

A few minutes later, her plate arrived. But instead of scrambled eggs, there was an omelette. She politely asked if they could bring her scrambled eggs instead. No problem, said the server, taking the plate back to the kitchen.

In super-fast time, a perfectly moulded pile of scrambled eggs appeared. But there was something… off.

It didn't look quite right. It didn't taste quite right.

And then she realised, this wasn't scrambled eggs, it was her omelette! They had taken the original omelette, finely chopped it, pressed it into a mould, added a garnish and sent it back out.

When she questioned this, they initially denied it – their story was they were freshly scrambled eggs. But we knew they weren't. So she asked someone else. Sure enough, the truth came out, the chef was busted and in that moment our trust in the restaurant collapsed.

And it wasn't about the eggs. It was about being lied to.

Small Lies = Big Problems

A lot of businesses think that small cheats don't matter.

But they do. Because your customers aren't stupid.

A tiny deception might seem harmless in the moment, but it creates long-term damage that businesses never fully recover from. Here are some of the most common ways businesses cheat their customers and why they always backfire:

Fake reviews – Trying to boost a company's reputation with phoney testimonials or deleting bad reviews. The second customers realise a business is doing this, trust is gone.

Hidden fees – Advertising one price, but charging more at checkout. This might win a short-term sale, but customers won't come back.

Cutting corners – Reusing food (like the scrambled egg incident), swapping products, using cheaper materials but still charging the same. Customers notice changes and they don't like being deceived.

Overcharging and staying silent – If a customer accidentally overpays, the right thing to do is refund the difference. Keeping quiet might seem like an easy win, but it's stealing.

Lying about stock or delivery times – 'Your order is on the way!' when it isn't. 'We have it in stock' when you don't. The greatest of all, taxis, 'He's just round the corner.' Customers hate being misled.

All of these seem small in the moment. But they create massive long-term damage.

When Lies Cost Millions

It might start as a little white lie, a simple shortcut or a way to cover up a mistake. But history has shown that deception, no matter how minor it seems at first, can spiral into disaster; costing millions and destroying reputations. Remember these?

Volkswagen Emissions Scandal (2015)

VW installed software to cheat emissions tests, making their diesel cars appear cleaner than they were. When the truth came out, Volkswagen faced over $30 billion in fines, legal battles and plummeting customer trust.

Post Office Horizon Scandal (2000-2014)

One of the UK's biggest miscarriages of justice. Hundreds of innocent sub-postmasters were wrongly accused of theft due to a faulty IT system, while the Post Office denied any issues. The fallout was over £130 million in legal costs and an £816 million compensation scheme, not to mention irreparable reputational damage.

Wells Fargo Fake Accounts Scandal (2016)

To meet sales targets, employees secretly opened millions of fake accounts. The result was a $3 billion fine, a meteoric drop in customer trust and long-term brand damage.

Enron (2001)

The energy giant hid its financial losses through fraudulent accounting. Once exposed, Enron collapsed overnight, taking thousands of jobs and billions in investments with it.

These weren't just mistakes. They were deliberate deceptions that destroyed businesses and I bet you know a local example or something you've been caught up in too.

Why Honesty Is Hard (But Always Best)

Admitting a mistake feels painful in the short term. No one likes telling a customer bad news.

But what's worse? Lying about it, getting caught and destroying trust completely.

Think about the scrambled eggs incident. If the waiter had said something like: *'I'm so sorry about that! The chef's made omelette eggs – that's a new one on me. Let us make you some fresh scrambled eggs'.* It would have been fine.

Mistakes happen. Customers understand and forgive quickly. But they don't forgive and forget dishonesty.

The Right Way: Owning Up

Here's the thing: honesty doesn't just prevent damage. It builds loyalty.

Imagine a company overcharged you by accident. Instead of hoping you don't notice, they immediately call to apologise and refund the difference.

You're now more loyal than before. Because you've seen firsthand that the company does the right thing – even when no one's watching.

Or think about stock issues. A business could say, 'It'll be with you next week' (even though it won't). Or they could say, 'We're sorry, but it's going to take longer than expected. We can offer you a refund, a similar product or you could wait until it's in stock. What would you prefer?'

Customers will always respect honesty over false promises, no matter how well-intentioned.

Ripple Effect

Honesty Creates Loyalty. One lie, one broken promise, one moment of deception and bad news spreads fast. Suddenly, a business isn't just losing one customer. They're losing everyone that customer tells.

Honesty spreads too.

When you do the right thing, even when it's hard, customers talk about that too. They tell their friends. They leave great reviews. They stay loyal. It's the difference between short-term deception and long-term loyalty. And you'll feel good.

So please don't cheat. Because even if the customer doesn't know, you do.

19

Laughing Together

The power of humour in customer service

Recently, Christine and I checked into a hotel where we were presenting the next day. They'd given us a large room to prepare for the event. All seemed well – until we heard it. A strange scratching noise from the ceiling. Christine's first thought? Rats. My first thought? Take out my phone and record the sound.

We immediately went to reception, played the video (shocked faces) and asked for another room. Of course, the hotel was fully booked and the engineer had gone home. Instead, they sent the head housekeeper to check it out. Not exactly the expert I was hoping for.

In comes Veronica, a cheerful lady, ready to tackle our problem with a smile. Picture the scene: Veronica, my wife and I standing under the ceiling, listening for the mysterious noise.

Then, it happened. *Scritch-scratch, scritch-scratch.*

Veronica let out a shriek so loud that my wife and I jumped. The three of us stood there, momentarily startled. Then, the absurdity of the situation hit us and Veronica started to laugh. Within seconds we were all howling.

It turned out there were no rats in the ceiling. The culprit was a leaking AC pipe. And while that wasn't ideal, the laughter we shared with Veronica turned the situation from a potential complaint into a moment we'll never forget. Veronica's ability to 'read the room' and her use of self-deprecating humour (at the right time) transformed what could have been a frustrating experience into a positive one.

When Laughter Misses

But humour can't solve everything. If used at the wrong time, it will have the opposite effect. Here's another hotel experience – this one also involved laughter, but not from me.

My wife, our two young children and I were staying at a hotel in glorious Glasgow. We were exhausted and were taking an afternoon nap when boom, the fire alarm went off. Now, when a fire alarm goes off and you've got children with you, as much as you'd like to stay calm, panic kicks in. We scrambled to get the kids, grabbed our basic things and headed down the internal fire escape. To make matters worse, as we descended, we could smell burning. And the lower we got, the stronger the smell.

Naturally, we assumed the worst. By the time we reached the ground floor, my heart was pounding, my wife was on edge and the kids were shaken. For all we knew, the hotel was in flames.

But as we stepped into the foyer, we were greeted not by firemen, but by the general manager, let's call him Edward, who looked at us, and – to our disbelief – started laughing.

'Don't worry,' he said between chuckles, 'It's just some work in the basement. Someone got a bit too enthusiastic cutting a pipe and they've set off the alarm. No fire here!'

Then Edward laughed again and said, 'Oh, the look on your faces!'

And this is where his idea of humour and our idea of humour had, let's say a mis-match. We were not in the mood for jokes. We were furious. I ended up shouting at him, livid at how casually he'd handled the situation. Not only had we been terrified, but now we were being laughed at. That was thirty years ago and it still sticks with me.

Funny Right And Funny Wrong

Two experiences, both in hotels with paying guests, two sides to using humour in customer service. On the one hand, humour can be an excellent way to ease tension and turn a problem into something positive. On the other? Angry guests who still bang on about it 30 years later.

How do you find funny right and avoid funny wrong? Here are some simple takeaways for using humour the right way:

Know Your Audience

Not everyone will appreciate the same kind of humour. Veronica could tell we were the type of people who could laugh with her. Edward? Not so much. Read the room before trying to be funny.

Timing Is Everything

The biggest difference between these two stories? Timing. Veronica's laugh came after the problem had been discovered and the tension had been broken. Edward's laughter came at the height of our panic, which magnified the situation and made it much worse.

Keep It Light

Humour should never be at the customer's expense. Laughing at our frightened faces was not Edward's smartest move. Humour should always be inclusive, bringing people together rather than bringing them down.

Humour Enhances, It Doesn't Solve

Humour can make a tough situation more bearable, but it shouldn't be mistaken for the solution. Veronica still addressed the issue (the leak), I've no idea how she did it, but she found us another room in the full hotel. While eager Edward relied on humour instead of offering reassurance first.

Ripple Effect

Humour, when appropriate, creates positive ripples far beyond the initial interaction. At the right time and in the right moment the ripple effect of laughter is glorious. It's contagious.

When someone leaves an interaction feeling good, they're more likely to share that feeling with others. Maybe they'll tell the story to a friend or share it with colleagues at work. Perhaps it'll turn into a story they tell time after time and write about in a brilliant customer service book. Thank you Veronica.

The ABC Of Using Humour In Customer Service

If there's one thing these stories show, it's that humour can be a powerful tool – but only when used thoughtfully. Here's a simple ABC on how you can use humour to create better customer experiences:

Appropriate the situation: Is the customer already stressed or upset? If so, humour might need to take a back seat until the problem is resolved.

Balanced: Humour should support your customer service efforts, not overshadow them. Solve the problem first, then use humour to lighten the mood.

Candid: Forced humour comes off as fake. If humour doesn't feel natural in the moment, skip it.

Laugh With, Not At

Humour can turn a difficult moment into a positive one. It can humanise your brand and create a connection that customers remember. But timing, tone and audience matter. Laugh with your customers, not at them. And remember, when used appropriately, laughter can be the most memorable part of your service.

20

Creating A Positive Environment

The real reason to smile

Have you ever walked into a room and just *felt* good? Perhaps it was the warm glow of natural light, the faint scent of lavender in the air or the infectious presence of someone who looked genuinely happy to be there. Creating a positive environment is service alchemy – it's the art of combining tangible and intangible elements to make a space *feel* good.

And this matters more than ever, because a positive environment doesn't just influence how customers feel – it inspires the people who occupy and work in it too. It's a virtuous cycle: happy staff create happy environments and happy environments make it easy for customers to feel brilliant too.

Here are ten ways to create a positive environment and find a *real* reason to smile.

1. **Aroma Advantage**

Science tells us that smells have a powerful link to emotions and memories. A subtle hint of citrus can make a space feel clean, while lavender promotes calm. Think of how luxury hotels pump signature scents into their lobbies – it's not an accident. In your environment, whether it's a shop, an office, a bus, or your home office, creating a pleasant aroma can immediately shift the mood.

2. Clean Spaces, Clear Minds

Let's be blunt: nothing kills a positive vibe faster than dirty toilets or messy workspaces. When an environment is spotless, it says, 'We care.' This isn't just for customers – it's for staff too. A clutter-free, clean space allows people to focus and feel valued.

3. Let There Be Light

Dim and dingy spaces make people feel... well, dim and dingy. Natural light works wonders for boosting energy, mood and productivity, but if that's not an option, consider warm, soft lighting. It's welcoming, flattering and far more inviting than the glare of harsh fluorescents.

4. Dress For Success

How you present yourself impacts how others feel about the environment you inhabit. A crisp uniform, a neat appearance and a genuine smile signals pride. And this can work in any business. When trucking giants Eddie Stobart introduced the wearing of ties for their drivers it was a sign that they were different, smarter and proud of it.

5. Presentation Is Everything

How you present... anything... yourself, your work, an idea or a product shapes how it's perceived. A polished presentation, a neatly designed report and the way a bag is handed to a customer speak volumes.

It's about care and pride. Let's take that bag. Throw something in and it devalues the product. Placing something in carefully and then passing it with attention and respect shows you value the product and the recipient.

Whether it's clean shoes (take a look at yours), a thoughtfully designed PowerPoint, or a well-wrapped product, a perfect presentation makes the recipient feel valued.

6. **Sounds Of Brilliance**

The soundtrack of a space can transform its atmosphere. Think of how a lively playlist energises a shop or how soft background music soothes a spa. Even in a call centre, managing noise levels and tone of voice can make the environment more pleasant for everyone.

7. **See The Signs**

Clear signage is a silent guide, it tells people where to go, what to do and what to expect without confusion. Well-placed, easy-to-read signs reduce stress, eliminate guesswork and make environments feel calm and organised.

I was looking for the loo in a small restaurant a while ago and ended up in the kitchen. When I apologised the friendly chef said, 'Don't worry, everyone does that'. I visited again a couple of years later... exactly the same.

Whether it's directional signs in a store, labels in a workspace, or a simple welcome message, great signage helps everyone feel at ease and in control.

8. **Thoughtful Touches, Big Impact**

Little things make environments memorable. A clean, nicely set table with napkins at a café. A cosy waiting area with new magazines. A jug of water and sparkling glasses in a meeting room. These small, thoughtful details show you care.

9. **Bring The Outside In**

Bringing greenery into a space boosts mood and reduces stress. Whether it's a plant on a desk or flowers in a reception area, a touch of nature works wonders.

Smile Stat

A study published in the Journal of Physiological Anthropology found that interaction with indoor plants can reduce both physiological and psychological stress.

10. Make It Fun

Even the most serious environments can benefit from a little playfulness. Instead of clinical, cold spaces, with scary machines, the paediatric isolation rooms at Hospital Universitario La Paz in Madrid have been transformed into 'moon stations'. Panels were added to blend with the machines and designed to look like spacecraft controls with backlit features that emulate lunar light. It's a way to turn daunting hospital stays into exciting adventures.

Creating a positive environment doesn't happen by accident. It's about deliberate choices – the smells, the sounds, the smiles. And it begins with the people who work there. When your team feels brilliant, they'll create an environment that makes customers want to come back again and again.

Take a moment to look around. Smell the air. Listen to the sounds. Feel the vibe. Ask yourself: is this a place that makes people smile?

21

Trust Me:

I'm A Customer Service Expert

In customer service, trust isn't just nice to have – it's your currency. Without it, you're chasing transactions. With it, you're building relationships. Trust isn't demanded, it's earned and when you've earned it, everything is easier.

But building trust doesn't happen by accident. It's built intentionally, through every interaction, every promise kept and every moment of listening.

Emotional Bank Account

Trust is the key currency of the *Emotional Bank Account*. Every customer interaction is an opportunity for a deposit or a withdrawal.

Meet their expectations? That's a credit. Go above and beyond? That's a big deposit. Ignore their concerns, overpromise, or fail to deliver? That's a withdrawal. And withdrawals hurt more than deposits help.

Your goal isn't just to avoid a negative balance. It's to create so much trust that, even when something goes wrong (and it will), the balance of your emotional bank account can absorb it.

Why Listening Is Everything

When you listen – really listen – you tell your customers, 'I see you. You matter.'

But most people don't listen to understand. They listen to respond. And customers know the difference.

If you want to build trust, do this: Stop what you're doing and give your full attention. Reflect on what you've heard: 'So what you're saying is...' Then ask more questions that show you care. My go-to phrase is, 'Tell me more…'.

Listening isn't a tactic. It's a trust-building gift.

See Chapter 30 The Secret Language Of Listening for much more on this.

Why We Don't Trust (And How To Fix It)

Scepticism is built into us. It's a survival tool. We don't trust because we've been burned before.

Your customers, past, present and future, have been over-promised, undervalued and let down. They're cautious and rightly so.

To overcome that scepticism, you must do what others won't. Trust isn't built by grand gestures, it's built in the moments that may seem small at the time but they aren't.

Here are my top ten trust builders:

Be transparent: If there's a problem and it's affecting what you can do, tell your customer.

Don't exaggerate: If it's going to take five days, say five – not four.

Follow through: Do what you said you'd do, every… single… time.

Accept mistakes: When you mess up (and you or someone else will), own it. Apologise sincerely. Fix it.

Stay proactive: Don't wait for customers to chase you for updates. Keep them informed at every step of the process.

Show empathy: Acknowledge frustrations. Put yourself in their shoes. Make your customer feel understood. Not just heard.

Take Ownership: Even if it's not your fault. Blaming others doesn't build trust, but taking ownership and finding a solution does.

Be Consistent: This takes time: be reliable. Not once, not twice, every time.

Be Real: Drop the corporate jargon. Be human. Humans trust humans.

Keep Calm and Carry On: If you can stay calm under fire when things go wrong (and they will), your reaction will matter more than the problem itself.

Ripple Effect

Here's the magic of trust: it doesn't just stay with one person. It ripples.

A trusted customer tells the people they trust. Their friends tell their friends. Trust grows and slowly spreads, but it all starts with you. Your words, your actions, your care.

So trust me on this. If you want loyal customers, you don't need gimmicks or tricks. You need trust. Build it, nurture it and above all, when you've got it, protect it. Because when trust is there, everything else falls into place.

22

It's Not You, It's Me

This isn't just the world's worst way of being dumped – it's fundamental when it comes to customer service.

You can't control other people. You can't stop customers from being rude, colleagues from being difficult, or your boss from piling on the pressure… But you can control how you react.

That's the difference between someone who constantly feels stressed and overwhelmed and someone who stays calm and in control – even in tough situations.

In customer service, it's easy to blame a bad interaction on *them.* 'They were impossible,' 'They were rude,' 'They just didn't get it.'

But here's a truth bomb. The problem isn't them. It's you and how you respond.

Jenny's Café

Jenny, a café owner, had been running on empty. She needed a break, so she asked, Alice, who normally worked Saturdays, to manage things while she took a well-earned holiday.

When Jenny returned a week later, refreshed and tanned, she asked Alice, 'How did it go?'

'Mostly great,' Alice said. 'But there was one customer who was just awful. Difficult, grumpy, impossible to please.'

Jenny was surprised. She prided herself on knowing her regulars, and in her mind, they were all lovely. But later that morning, Alice nudged her. 'Here he is.'

Jenny turned, expecting a storm cloud of a man. Instead, she saw Charles, a long-time customer, walking in with a warm smile. Charles was the perfect regular, he'd order his coffee and cake, chat briefly and leave a generous tip.

Jenny was stunned. 'Him? That's who you had trouble with?'

Alice nodded, confused. So they talked, trying to work out what had gone wrong. Eventually, it clicked. On Alice's second day, the café was packed and seats were short. As Charles had been sitting alone, she'd walked over and asked, 'Mind if I take this chair?'

But what Alice didn't know was that Charles had come to the café every day with his wife Sarah and she had passed away just a few months ago. The chair Alice had taken wasn't spare, it was Sarah's.

Alice's stomach dropped. She hadn't meant to upset him, she simply hadn't known.

She looked across the café. Charles was still there, finishing his coffee. She walked over and this time asking permission first, sat down. They talked and within minutes, Alice realised: Charles wasn't grumpy. He was grieving.

The Big Shift – Taking Responsibility For Your Reactions

Visualise this: One (difficult) customer – two employees. One lets frustration take over. They get defensive, their tone sharpens and suddenly, the situation escalates. The customer pushes back harder and it becomes a battle.

The other employee stays calm. They listen. They don't take the customer's attitude personally. And instead of making the situation worse, they use their skills to defuse it.

Same customer. Same problem. Different reaction – different result.

Your reaction determines whether a situation gets better or worse. That's why taking responsibility for how you respond is one of the most powerful skills you can develop.

The Science Of Emotional Control

Psychological research on *emotional regulation* shows that people who manage their emotions effectively experience less stress, make better decisions and have stronger relationships.

Sciencey Bit 

A study by Dr. James Gross at Stanford University found that people who reframe negative experiences, choosing to see them in a more neutral or positive light, reduce their stress levels and improve their ability to handle difficult situations.

This is why the best customer service professionals don't take things personally. They see a difficult customer not as a personal attack, but as a problem to solve.

And when you can do that, you become unshakeable.

How To Master Your Reactions

Pause before reacting – When something triggers you, take a breath before responding. That tiny pause between stimulus and reaction can be the difference between reacting emotionally and responding thoughtfully.

Reframe the situation. Lead with curiosity, not judgement – If someone is being difficult, get curious. Ask questions. 'What's actually going on here?' People often just want to be heard.

Use emotional detachment – Don't let someone else's bad mood become your bad mood. Their attitude is about them, not you.

Customer Service Is Your Training Camp, Real Life Is The Battleground

Handling awkward customers, demanding bosses and challenging service situations is the best training you'll ever receive.

If you can master staying calm, asking the right questions and controlling your reactions with clients, imagine how powerful you'll be when it comes to difficult conversations in your personal life, managing conflict, or leading a team.

It's not you, it's me isn't just about handling work challenges – it's about building a skill that makes your life easier, happier and more successful in every area.

23

Loyalty 4.0

In my book *5 Star Service*, the opening chapter in part one (The Psychology of Service), talks about creating Loyalty 3.0

Loyalty 1.0 is built on the simple premise that you do what you say you will do.

Loyalty 2.0 is you do what your customer wants you to do – be customer driven.

Loyalty 3.0 argues the importance of customer service being part of the DNA of your organisation. It's not something that you do alongside your business, it's integral to every part.

Now we have Loyalty 4.0 and the bar has been raised again. Loyalty 4.0 is recognising and providing for the unexpressed needs of your customer. That means providing a level of service that your customer didn't know they wanted or needed until you introduced and provided it.

The new level of recognising and rewarding loyal customers is crucial. And yes, I know loyalty is a two-way street; for you to be loyal to your customers you want your customers to be loyal to you.

And yet there's still a temptation to focus on gathering new business at the expense of the old. When I see a special offer with the small print saying it's for 'new customers only', I feel a little peeved. Especially if I've been loyal to that particular brand for years.

Some companies do it well. I've been buying my gas and electricity through *Octopus Energy* for many years. They keep me up to date, offer me the best deals and because I'm a loyal customer they give me a chance, once a month, to *spin the wheel.* I've never won but it doesn't matter, because the opportunity to win £1,000, £100 or even £1 is a nod to my loyalty.

I've had the same favourite restaurant in Newcastle for over 30 years. Others have come and gone; I've been given special offers, wooed by Michelin stars and tempted by the latest fancy frippery. But when we want certainty, a meal cooked with care, made from quality ingredients and served in a comfortable friendly environment, there's only one place to go, *21 Newcastle.*

Loyal customers are the backbone of any successful venture. They not only provide repeat business but often become brand advocates, bringing in new customers through word-of-mouth and personal recommendation.

However, if these loyal customers feel neglected, they will quickly switch to your competitors. Recognising and rewarding loyalty helps build strong, long-term relationships that are beneficial to both the customer and the business.

One more? I've had the same hairdresser since I was 20. I've followed Richard Watts (remember him from Chapter 13?) around the North East. My loyalty is such that when I lived in Glasgow I would drive over 100 miles to get a haircut.

Is he a particularly good hairdresser? I *think* so, but let's just say it's more about the relationship than the haircuts. His scissor skills are decent, but it's our relationship that keeps me loyal.

Richard charges £35 for a haircut. I visit 12 times a year and I've been a client for 35 years. The lifetime value so far (and I know he wasn't always £35) is around £14,700. The way he hikes his prices up [joking Richard] that could double in the next ten years.

Yes, loyalty is valuable.

Some Practical Steps To Recognise And Reward Loyal Customers:

Identify Your Loyal Customers

Use your CRM system or AI to track customer purchases and identify those who return frequently. Look for patterns in their buying behaviour and segment your loyal customer base. I recently gave Brilliant Ai (my AI assistant) a spreadsheet with 11,500 transactions on it and asked for any trends or analysis. The results were amazing, identifying my top twenty customers and enabling me to give them something for their loyalty.

Create A Loyalty Programme

You don't have to be a supersized supermarket to develop a structured loyalty programme that rewards customers for repeat business. This could include points for purchases, exclusive discounts, early access to new products and special events.

Personalise Rewards

Tailor rewards to individual customer preferences. Personalised rewards make customers feel valued and appreciated. My eyes light up when I see an offer for something I genuinely want and need.

Celebrate Milestones

Recognise significant milestones such as anniversaries of their first purchase or reaching a certain number of transactions. Send personalised messages or gifts to mark these occasions.

Ask For And Act On Feedback

Regularly request feedback from your loyal customers and make visible efforts to implement their suggestions. This shows that you value their input and are committed to improving their experience. See Chapter 39 Feedback – The Gift You Didn't Ask For, for more on this.

Surprise And Delight

Occasionally surprise your loyal customers with unexpected rewards or experiences. This could be anything from a handwritten thank-you note to an exclusive invitation to a VIP event.

Ripple Effect

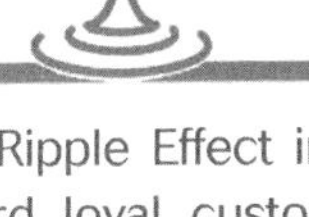

This is possibly the most obvious Ripple Effect in this book. If you recognise and reward loyal customers, those people will feel more valued. People who feel more valued are more likely to recommend and refer you.

24

No Bad Days

What to do when you don't want to smile

Even the most upbeat professionals have days when smiling feels like a Herculean task. It's normal. Life throws curveballs and sometimes those curveballs hit you right in the face.

But here's the kicker, it's rarely a bad day. More often it's a bad moment, one rough interaction or at the most an unfortunate hour.

No Bad Days

There's a great song by Macklemore called 'No Bad Days'. I challenge you to listen to it and not feel uplifted. It'll take 2 minutes and 50 seconds from your life and you'll thank me. The essence is about accepting the cards you've been dealt and choosing to make the very best of them. Go and listen to it now… or maybe do it after you've read this chapter.

The first step in having no bad days is understanding that labelling an entire day as 'bad' gives it more power than it deserves. Is it a bad day, or was it just a difficult meeting, a missed deadline or a snappy customer? By reframing your perspective, you can keep a negative experience from casting a shadow over the entire day.

At any moment you are in a particular 'state'. It could be a happy state, frustrated state, a curious state, a bewildered state, a sad state or a dozen other states.

One thing I'm certain of is the state you are in now is not the same state you will be in this time tomorrow. Usually, your state is dictated by external events. Something happens, you react and your state changes. But what if it was the other way around?

State Changing

I love sharing the State Change Triangle as a way to show people how to get out of a funk.

The three sides of the triangle are:
Language, Focus and Physiology.

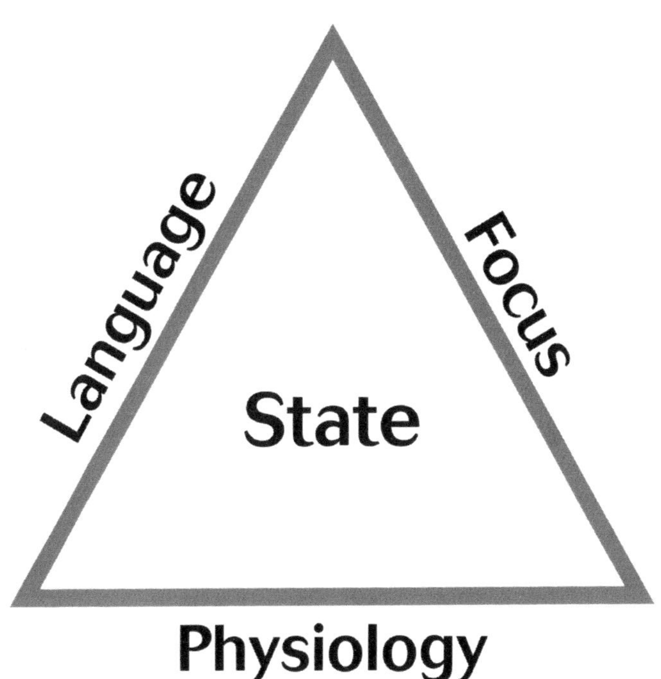

Language - The Emotional Impact Of Your Words

What you say, your choice of words and even the words you use to think. Words have a massive impact on how you feel.

Consider the language that you might use to describe a challenging situation with a customer. 'They're a nightmare.' 'Honestly, they were doing my head in.' And usually, there's a whole bunch of expletives to make it even more dramatic.

If your language is having a direct impact on how you feel (and we know it does), then doesn't it make sense to use some better, more helpful, language? With over a million words to choose from in the English language, I'm sure you can find something.

Focus - Where Attention Goes, Energy Flows

If you're looking for something bad, you will find it. If you choose to look at any situation, even the most positive ones and do it with a negative focus, it is possible to find something wrong. Some people specialise in this.

'Beautiful day, isn't it?'

'Yes, but it's going to rain later.'

The opposite is also true. You can look at any negative situation and if you change your focus, you can find something positive about it.

Another focus classic is when you're in a negative 'state' you tend to reflect on the past. You want to find out what went wrong, focus on finding someone to blame and trying to understand how the situation occurred. As much as this little pity party might appease your ego, it won't make you feel any better.

Instead, if you focus on the future; short-term or long-term and laser focus on to the positives you will feel better. And if you can't find anything immediately? One thing you can guarantee with any negative situation is, it will pass.

Physiology – Your Body Speaks First

This is what you do with your body. Breathing, where you look, your stance. You can tell some people are angry or upset before they've said a word. Others can bring joy into a room the second they walk through the door.

If you can pick up on others' physiology, doesn't it make sense that (as the closest person to your physiology) you pick up on yours too? Think about what you do with your physiology when you feel fantastic. Where are your shoulders? How do you breathe? What do you do with your facial muscles? Once you understand that combination, lock it in.

If you want to make an impact and experience a state change in seconds, it's powerful to exaggerate your physiology. Just for a couple of seconds. So rather than forcing a smirk, you might as well force a massive grin. Take some deeeeeep breaths, go for a huge cheesy smile, open your arms and feel the release of those energising endorphins that make you feel better.

Change Your State

If you change any one of these three things, you'll feel better. Change two and you're already halfway to creating a better emotional state. Change all three and you'll immediately feel different. And so will those around you.

I'm no advocate for being happy-clappy and throwing out trite statements like 'There are no problems, only opportunities', but I do know, having taught this technique to thousands of people and using it myself pretty much daily, that the best way to make sure you never have a bad day is to learn how to recognise when you're in an unhelpful state. Then change your language, focus and physiology. Do this and you'll instantly change your state.

Sciencey Bit

A fascinating piece of research by Prof. Gal Sheppes of Tel Aviv University found that Cognitive Reappraisal (what I call managing your state) is more effective than acceptance in the short term and significantly decreases negative emotions. In the longer term, acceptance has a bigger impact. Change your state in the short term and accept the situation in the long term.

And if the instant State Change Triangle technique isn't right for you, here are some other practical steps for tough times:

Take A Break

Step away from the situation for a few minutes. Breathe deeply, take a short walk, or practise a quick mindfulness exercise.

Connect With A Colleague

Talk to a supportive colleague or friend. Sometimes a fresh perspective is all you need to lighten your emotional load.

Focus On A Small Win (SWin)

Identify and celebrate small achievements throughout your day. This keeps you focused on what's going right instead of what's going wrong.

Practise Self-Compassion

Be kind to yourself. Acknowledge that it's okay to have a tough moment. Treat yourself with the same kindness and understanding you'd offer a friend.

Everyone has times when smiling feels impossible, but these situations don't have to define your day.

Remember, it's just a bad moment. NO BAD DAYS!

25

Trustomer Service

Instead of designing brilliant experiences for the best customers, many businesses build systems based on fear of the worst ones. They assume that if one person might steal, cheat, or lie – everyone will. And so, they create processes that punish everyone.

It's the reason why, when you go into some shops, you feel like a potential criminal rather than a valued customer.

It's also why businesses lose money.

Because trust isn't just a nice idea – it's good business. Those who get it right build stronger relationships, create loyal customers and ultimately make more sales.

The Over-Policed Customer

Have you ever been treated with suspicion when all you were trying to do was shop, eat, or spend your own money?

Here are some classic examples. And allow me a grrr and a dollop of sarcasm here:

Retail: I bought 36 bottles of water from Tesco. They were in heavy packs of six, so I lifted one onto the checkout. As he scanned it I told him I had six in total. The cashier leaned over and made a point of deliberately counting the remaining packs.

Fashion: Some shops still insist on customers leaving their belongings outside fitting rooms or limiting how many items they can try on. Is the assumption everyone plans to walk off in a stolen outfit?

Banking: The ultimate 'we don't trust you' experience. Banks seem to love blocking withdrawals from your own account or making it difficult to access your funds. Extra security is understandable, but when you have to justify a withdrawal, of your own money, to your bank, it just feels wrong.

Restaurants: Where the chef won't make a small change to a dish because 'that's not how it was intended'. Brilliant. The chef is now antagonising for a paying customer. Is that what was intended?

When customers don't feel trusted, they don't argue. They don't demand an explanation. They just leave. And they don't come back.

Trust Wins

Now let's flip it. Some businesses lean into trust and guess what? They win.

Amazon: When something isn't right, Amazon makes returns incredibly easy. As soon as you provide proof of postage, you immediately get your refund. They don't wait until they've received the item. That confidence in customers builds trust, and trust keeps people coming back and spending more.

Hotel Honesty Bars: Some hotels have bars where guests serve themselves and pay later. It sounds risky, but research shows that people are more honest when they feel trusted and guests who experience this are more likely to spend more and return.

Apple Stores: Have you noticed that Apple doesn't use security tags on its products? It's a subtle but powerful signal. They create an environment where customers feel welcome, rather than like suspects under surveillance.

Businesses that trust their customers create an atmosphere where customers trust them in return

The Reality Check - Balancing Trust And Security

Just to be clear: theft, fraud, and dishonesty exist. Retailers, banks, and businesses aren't paranoid. There are, and always will be, customers who take advantage. But the mistake is in assuming all customers are a problem just because some are.

There needs to be balance.

Yes, protect against fraud and theft. But don't punish genuine customers in the process.

Yes, set boundaries. But don't make rules that make customers feel unwelcome.

Make sure trusted customers get better experiences, not more obstacles.

Smile Stat 

A survey by PwC revealed that while 87% of executives believe customers highly trust their companies, in reality, only about 30% of consumers feel that way. This disparity highlights the trust gap between what execs believe and what consumers think.

Why You Don't Trust Customers And Why Customers Don't Trust You

And, because I'm full of hope, here's how to fix it.

Scepticism is built into us. It's a survival tool. We don't trust because we've been burned before.

Your customers, past, present and future, have been overpromised, undervalued and let down. They're cautious and rightly so. Why should they trust you?

Here are 10 ways to build trust with customers:

1. **Be Transparent** – If something goes wrong, don't hide it. Customers appreciate honesty, whether it's a delay, an issue with a product, or an unexpected change.

2. **Follow Through on Promises** – If you say you'll call back, call back. If you offer next-day delivery, make sure it arrives on time. Small broken promises chip away at trust.

3. **Empower Your Team** – Give employees the authority to make judgement calls instead of forcing them to follow rigid policies that frustrate them and your customers.

4. **Make Returns and Refunds Easy** – The fewer hoops your customers have to jump through, the more likely they are to buy from you again.

5. **Show Appreciation** – A simple thank-you email, a text, handwritten note, or a loyalty reward can go a long way towards making customers feel valued.

6. **Don't Over-Police** – If you have security measures in place, make sure they don't alienate honest customers. No one enjoys feeling like a suspect.

7. **Ask for Feedback – And Act on It** – Customers trust businesses that listen. If you collect feedback but never implement it, they'll notice.

8. **Give the Benefit of the Doubt** – If a long-time customer says their order never arrived or a meal wasn't right, believe them. The cost of replacing an item is small compared to the cost of losing their trust and future business.

9. **Personalise the Experience** – Use customer data wisely to tailor interactions. A business that remembers your name, preferences, or order history shows that they care.

10. **Lead with Trust** – Assume positive intent. When you trust your customers, they'll trust you in return and that leads to customer loyalty.

26

Are You Writing That Down?

You know the moment. You're in a restaurant, rattling off your order – starter, main, extra side, maybe a tweak to the dressing – when you realise the server is just looking and nodding.

'Should you be writing that down?', you ask. They nod, smile and assure you, *'I've got it!'*

You're thinking, '*No, you haven't.*'

And sure enough, when the food arrives, something is wrong. The extra sauce, the no-onion request or the worst, the side of fries is missing! The sheer predictability of it. All of this could have been avoided with one simple action: just write it down.

Why do some people resist using simple, reliable systems? Is it ego? Overconfidence? A belief that 'good service' means relying on memory alone? The best service comes from getting things *right*, not from attempting party tricks with client's orders.

Simple Systems, Brilliant Results

The best businesses don't just rely on memory or luck – they create systems that work. And they don't need to be flashy or complex. Sometimes, the most effective solutions are the simplest. Here are a few examples where a small, well-placed system makes a massive difference:

Taking Notes In Meetings

How often do people sit through meetings, nodding along, only to leave wondering, *What did we agree on?* Today AI-powered note-taking tools can record, transcribe and summarise discussions automatically, ensuring no detail is lost.

Voicemails That Say Something

A voicemail that simply says, *"I'm not available right now. Leave a message."* is the equivalent of shrugging at a customer.

A brilliant voicemail sets expectations:
"Hi, you've reached Michael. I'm unavailable until 3 pm, but if it's urgent, email my team at [email address]. Otherwise, leave a message and I'll get back to you."
Instant clarity, instant professionalism.

Out-Of-Office Replies That Do More Than State The Obvious

Compare:
'I'm out of the office until Monday.'

With:
'Hi. I'm away until Monday, but if you need something urgent, contact [Name] at [Email]. If it can wait, I'll get back to you as soon as I return. Have a brilliant weekend.'

One leaves the customer stranded. The other makes them feel heard.

Bin Day

I'd make it a law that council websites should have, 'When is bin day?', as the first option on the landing page of their website. And before you nod and agree, ask yourself, what are people looking for on your website and how easy is it for them to find it?

Queueing Systems That Work (And Don't)

Let's talk about Kings Cross taxi rank. A chaotic queuing system where there's space for six cabs, but only enough room for one fare at the front of the line.

I asked Mark Monroe aka *MarksTaxiLife* to give us the benefit of his experience. He advised that Paddington Station is the best as they can load a minimum of 4 taxis simultaneously. I know the British love to queue, but how can one rank be four times more efficient than another?

Checklists That Prevent

Pilots use checklists before every flight. Why? Because missing even a single step can be catastrophic. In customer service, a simple checklist can mean the difference between a flawless experience and an awkward oversight. Hotels that use checklists for room preparation rarely miss a towel or a box of tissues. Restaurants that use checklists for orders rarely forget an allergy request.

Booking Confirmations That Remove Doubt

Have you ever booked something and then wondered, *Did that go through?* A simple confirmation email or text removes any doubt. Dentists, hair salons, car services – if they confirm bookings and send a reminder before the appointment, customers feel reassured and are less likely to be a no-show.

Clear Signage That Avoids Confusion

How many times have you walked into a business and thought, *Where do I go?* Shops with sections clearly marked, airports with intuitive signs and car parks with obvious exits make life so much easier. A well-placed sign can remove a hundred unnecessary questions.

Menus That Make Sense

Have you ever read a menu and thought, *What on earth does that mean?* Some places try too hard to be clever. A menu that's easy to read, with clear descriptions, makes ordering a pleasure. And when dietary information is clearly marked, it removes the awkwardness of having to ask.

Simple Wins - Every Time

The best businesses aren't the ones with the most complex systems; they're the ones with the smartest, *simplest* ones. A clear process removes doubt, speeds things up and makes life easier for everyone.

So, the next time someone asks, *'Are you writing that down?'* just wave your pen.

27

Getting The Balance Right

Professional and Friendly

The sweet spot between professionalism and friendliness can be a game-changer in customer service. Too much friendliness can feel intrusive, while excessive professionalism can seem cold.

Union Square Café in New York is renowned for its exceptional service, or as Founder, Danny Meyer calls it 'Enlightened Hospitality'. I recommend Union Square Café to EVERYONE who is visiting New York. The staff there are the masters of balancing banter and professionalism.

One friend thanked me and sent me this.

> LOVED Union Square Michael! As soon as our waiter knew we were from the North of England and we were Newcastle supporters, he chipped in with friendly banter. But never overstepped the mark, just read our cues perfectly.
>
> The food was outstanding, the service was a perfect balance between ability and affability, but our lasting impression was the brilliant 'bants'.

When Friendliness Goes Too Far And Formal Feels Forced

Gosh, it's a thin line. We've all had times when over-friendliness can become problematic. Have you experienced a well-meaning waiter who tries too hard to be your friend? Constant interruptions, personal anecdotes and forced jokes become overwhelming very quickly.

Then there's the flip side. Do you remember when fine dining used to be 'all about the food'? Silent staff would lurk ninja-like around the dining room, serving dishes with explanations that sounded like they'd had a thesaurus for breakfast.

And before you think it's just restaurants that do this, I've experienced meetings with financial advisors who thought they should be doing a stand-up routine, when all I wanted was practical, professional, financial advice.

What about the call centre rep who for some reason decides to call you 'buddy' or 'mate'? I often feel like saying, 'I'm not your mate! You don't know me.'

And don't get me started on Emojis!

The Importance Of Balance – Affable vs Authoritarian

Customers appreciate friendly interactions, but they also value professionalism. If you have knowledge and it's shared with the right amount of authority, customers appreciate that. Overstep the mark and your new friend might just turn into a foe.

Sciencey Bit

A meta-analysis published in Frontiers in Psychology examined factors influencing interpersonal trust and found that both competence (professionalism) and warmth (personability) are critical in building trust. The study concluded that individuals are more likely to trust others who demonstrate a combination of competence and warmth.

How To Strike The Perfect Balance

Read Social Cues

Pay attention to body language and verbal cues. If a customer seems engaged, a friendly approach works. If they appear more standoffish, a more professional demeanour might be better. This ties back to the SEE principle from the first part of this book.

Start With Professionalism

Make your very first interaction a professional one. This sets the tone and allows you to gauge your customer's response. If they respond positively, you can gradually introduce a more friendly informal element. This is the opposite of what many 'professionals' do, presenting themselves at your initial encounter as your 'best mate'.

Personalise Your Approach

Tailor your interaction based on your customer. Some may appreciate a chatty service, while others prefer minimal interaction. Use past experiences and customer profiles to inform your approach.

Maintain Boundaries

Friendly doesn't mean familiar. Maintain a level of formality and respect, addressing customers appropriately and showing consideration of their personal space. Avoid overly personal questions or comments.

Use Humour Carefully

A well-placed joke or light-hearted comment can enhance the interaction, but avoid forced humour. It should feel natural and appropriate to the situation and should NEVER be at the expense of your customer. See Chapter 19.

Ask For Feedback

Encourage feedback on your service style. This helps you understand what your customers prefer and allows you to adjust your approach accordingly.

According to Gallup, 85% of customers say a friendly and professional demeanour significantly impacts their customer service experience.

Real World Examples

21 Newcastle

For me, this is the perfect balance between professionalism and playfulness. It was at my favourite Newcastle restaurant, *21*. Yep them again. I was there with my mate for a lad's lunch; this was the interaction between us and our waiter when he came to take our order.

'OK, gentlemen. How's it going over here?'

'Perfect, we know what we want.'

'Excellent. Do we have it?'

He'd already made us smile and created instant rapport.

'Yes.' I replied.

'Phew, you could have caused some problems in the kitchen! What will it be?'

That's witty, entertaining and perfectly gauged.

Milestone Hotel, Kensington

Everything about The Milestone is glorious, but the breakfast is magical. Listening to staff claim Eggs Benedict is 'The breakfast of champions' and a cheeky waiter whispering to a wide-eyed 10-year-old, 'That's what Harry Potter orders when he stays here', is a delight.

Amazon Telephone Support

Taking into account that Amazon consider it 'a fault' if you need to speak to a human, when you do 99% of the time it's a joy. Mainly because they are empowered.

Jet2

I fell out with Jet2 over a mis-sold holiday a few years ago, but I forgave them after recent conversations with two customer service agents. They have the perfect balance of technical know-how and British banter. Yes, they talk about the weather, yes they're empowered and yes they've respectfully fixed MY mistakes.

Ripple Effect

Balancing professionalism and friendliness not only enhances customer satisfaction, but also improves employee morale. When staff are empowered to interact authentically and appropriately, it creates a positive work environment. Customers who experience this balance are more likely to return and recommend you and your business.

28

Are You Getting Too Much Recognition?

It's worth starting this chapter with a reminder of my definition of a customer. It's anyone who isn't you. That's a lot of people. And if you were to ask any of them if they believe they are getting too much recognition, you'd have a resounding no.

You know where this chapter's going.

Why Recognition Matters

I love being complimented on my choices. When a waiter or waitress says, 'Good choice' while I'm ordering a meal, even though deep down I'm aware they probably say that to everyone, there's still part of me that thinks, 'Thanks for recognising my amazing ability to choose a curry.' A thank you costs nothing. A genuine compliment takes seconds. And yet, in a world where we're all busier than ever, recognition is often the first thing to be forgotten.

The best way to build trust, loyalty and motivation isn't with big, sweeping gestures. It's the small, consistent moments of acknowledgement that can make a difference. And recognition is perfect for that.

Sciencey Bit

Studies show that people who feel recognised are:
More engaged in their work.
More likely to stay loyal to a business.
Happier, more motivated, and perhaps most importantly more likely to *pass that positivity on.*

When someone feels valued, they don't just work harder – they *care* more. That can make the difference between a transactional moment and an unforgettable experience.

Who Deserves More Recognition?

Recognition isn't just for those at the top, your most valued customer or employee of the month. It's for *everyone* who contributes – often in ways we don't always notice.

Customers – They chose you! They could have gone elsewhere, but they didn't. Recognise them and turn a one-time buyer into a lifelong fan.

Colleagues – It's easy to assume people *know* they're doing a good job. But a simple appreciative 'I noticed that' can transform workplace morale.

Your Boss – They're the first to hear complaints when things go wrong but rarely receive appreciation when things go right. Try thanking them – it's powerful.

Suppliers – The unsung heroes behind the scenes. Without them, businesses don't run. When was the last time you told them you appreciated their reliability?

Cheerleaders – The people who recommend you, who spread the word, who send customers your way. A little recognition goes a long way in making them feel valued.

Friends & Family – The ones who support you, usually without expecting anything in return. Do they know you appreciate them?

How To Give Genuine Recognition

The best recognition isn't generic. It's specific, thoughtful and personal.

Be Specific – Instead of 'Great job!', say, 'I appreciate how you handled that difficult situation with patience and professionalism.'

Public vs Private Recognition – Some people love a shout-out in front of others. Some prefer a quiet thank-you. Know your audience.

Go Beyond Words – A small note, a thoughtful gesture, or a simple reward can make all the difference.

Christine's Recognition Ritual

When we stay in a hotel, Christine always leaves a tip for the housekeeper. But she doesn't just leave money she writes a note. Not a generic 'Thank you,' but something specific:

> 'The bathroom was sparklingly clean.'
> 'Your turndown service was amazing.'
> 'The room felt so fresh and clean when we walked in. It was perfect.'

She writes it on the front of the envelope with the tip inside. She knows that a handwritten note saying *why* you appreciate someone means as much as the tip itself.

Time and time again we've seen the impact: Sometimes a thank you note is left in return, or the room feels like extra care has been taken. Often someone will thank her in the corridor. It's a small act that means everything.

Put the spotlight on your customer

Your customers don't just want service, they want to feel valued. I think the only limit to how you do this is your imagination, but here are a few ideas to get you started.

A thank you – A simple, genuine thank you could be the only thanks that person receives that day.

VIP – A little VIP treatment goes a long way. Have you ever been upgraded at a hotel or on a plane? It's brilliant!

Wee WOW™ – It needn't be big. A coffee shop remembering a regular and giving them an 'extra shot' on the house.

Handwritten... anything! – Thank-you notes, birthday cards, messages on a sticky note... recognition is made extra special when it's handwritten. In a world where 90% is on screen and the rest is printed, handwritten feels special.

Turning Recognition into a Competitive Advantage – Businesses that make customers feel seen *win.*

Mistakes People Make With Recognition

Thinking it's only for big achievements – The little, everyday efforts matter just as much.

Waiting too long – Recognition is best when it happens in the moment. We once had a client who held an 'annual recognition night'. You could have been the star employee the next day and then have to wait 364 days for your moment.

Making it about you – A proper thank-you has focus. It isn't 'I appreciate you because I couldn't have done it without you.' It's about them and what they do.

Forgetting to do it at all – The biggest mistake? Assuming people *know* they're appreciated. They don't – until you tell them. And if they do know, tell them again. Remember NO ONE IS GETTING TOO MUCH RECOGNITION.

A Challenge

Who can you recognise today? Could you share five moments of recognition with five different people? Think how that will make them feel. Think how it will make you feel.

Say Hello

29

Say Hello

Communication is one of, if not the, most important aspects of brilliant customer service. From having a quick chat to sending a detailed email, distributing a newsletter to knowing what to write in a card, developing your website copy to sharing words of encouragement, from what to write on a sign to creating copy for a sales pitch, it's all valuable.

Communication is key.

At a base level simply saying hello to your customer before they say hello to you is a brilliant challenge that I would encourage you to test. But saying 'hello' can be interpreted in many different ways.

This is the largest section of this book and for good reason. In this section of *See, Smile, Say Hello* we're going to go deeper. We'll explore the multiple ways you communicate and how you can make your communication better for your customers, your colleagues and yourself. Plus we'll have a chat with AI and discover how to brilliantly communicate when it all goes wrong.

30

The Silent Language Of Listening

In the cacophony of our modern world, rather than speaking louder – listen better. To stand out, try hearing the unsaid, understanding the undercurrents and connect through listening.

Fancy a deep dive into the gritty, unglamorous art of listening? Would you like to know how to ask the right questions, find your *inner Finn* and tune in to the silence that speaks volumes?

That's a flowery way of saying: talk less, listen more. Here's how.

Why Listening Matters

Let's start with *Active Listening*. It's one of those phrases that's easy for me to write, easier for you to read but challenging for us all to do. We all think we're good at it, but the reality is you (and me) could be better.

Listening isn't just a skill; it's a lifeline. It's about respect and trust and it's probably the best way to create a deeper human connection. When you listen, you make people feel seen, heard and valued. It's the difference between a superficial moment and a meaningful interaction.

So why don't we do it?

The science behind why we don't listen is fascinating and multi-layered, involving brain function, attention span and emotional response. Here's why we struggle:

Cognitive Overload

Brains are constantly bombarded with information – emails, texts, conversations, social media notifications – you name it. This 24/7 bombardment puts you in a state of *cognitive overload*, where your brain is simply juggling too much at once. Your prefrontal cortex, which handles decision-making and focus, gets overwhelmed and you lose the ability to fully engage in the conversation.

This is also known as 'Having a brain fart'.

Listening Fatigue

The concept of *listening fatigue* comes into play when you're in prolonged conversations or consuming a lot of auditory information. Your brain gets tired from processing all of those sound waves into meaning. Especially if it's complex or emotionally charged. This can cause you to 'mentally check out' even when you're physically present.

This is also known as, 'Yes dear, of course I'm listening.'

Selective Attention

Your brain naturally tunes out unimportant or repetitive information. It's not your fault! It's a survival mechanism – *selective attention*. From an evolutionary perspective, it makes sense: we focus on what seems most important for our survival.

In today's context this means you might filter out people's words if they don't seem immediately relevant to you – even if they are. Your brilliant brain is constantly scanning for what's most engaging, rather than taking it all in.

This is also known as 'I totally heard half of that.'

Your Brain's Processing Speed

Here's an interesting fact: the average person speaks at around 125 – 150 words per minute, but our brains can process up to 800 words per minute. This mismatch creates spare 'brain power' and that's where you tend to drift off. Your brilliant mind wanders because it can handle many more words than are being spoken. You start filling the gaps – thinking about the past, future, or that pizza you're having for dinner.

This is also known as, 'Thinking fast, but listening slow'.

Emotional Biases And Ego

Sometimes you don't listen because we're filtering everything through *emotional biases* – your ego! You're too busy thinking about how the conversation affects *you* rather than listening to understand. If you're preoccupied with defending your opinions or waiting for your turn to speak, you stop actively listening. Psychologically, this is good old *confirmation bias,* where you only focus on the bits that confirm your existing beliefs.

This is also known as 'You'll hear what you want to hear'.

Multitasking Myth

Many people believe they can multitask – scroll through their phone and listen to a meeting, all while making plans for the weekend and thinking, 'What's for tea?' (it's pizza). However, research shows that multitasking is a myth. What's happening is *task-switching,* where the brain rapidly flips between tasks, reducing your ability to concentrate deeply on any one thing. When you try to do two things at once, like listening and checking Instagram, you're not truly listening at all.

This is also known as, 'Working from home'.

The Willpower Factor

Psychologist Kelly McGonigal talks about *willpower being a finite resource.* You start the day with a certain amount and you use it up making decisions, resisting temptations and staying focused. It doesn't take long before you run out of the willpower required to listen attentively. By the time someone important needs you to focus, your willpower tank is drained and you can't fully engage.

This is also known as 'Tell me about your day'.

Sciencey Bit

Research by Zenger Folkman (I know cool business name) shows that leaders who listen well are more trusted and effective. This isn't touchy-feely stuff; it's hardcore strategy. Listening is power.

Some Practical Steps To Master The Art Of Listening

Be Present

Kill the distractions. Turn off your phone. Shut the laptop (unless you're using it for the actual communication). Be there completely.

Ask Open-Ended Questions

Dig deeper. 'Can you tell me more?'
'That's interesting, how did you discover that?'

Reply, Clarify And Rectify

Ask for details and repeat what you've heard.
'Can you walk me through what happened?'
'So, you're saying...'
'Here's what I can do...'

Boost Your Body Language

Show you're engaged. Nod, make eye contact, lean in.

Resist The Urge To Interrupt

Bite your tongue. Let them finish. Interrupting is the fastest way to kill a conversation.

Mental Replay

Rerun what you are hearing in your head. Not only will this clarify what's being said, but it will also use some of your brain's untapped processing power.

The temptation, when a customer complains, is to immediately fix the problem. To genuinely hear your customer, do this: First listen to their story, then ensure you understand the true issue before graciously fixing the problem and allowing your customer to have the final word.

Be More Finn

The Finns are more comfortable with silence during conversation. Silence is not considered as awkward or uncomfortable in Finland as it might be in other cultures. Instead, it's respected as a natural part of communication. This creates space for listening and understanding.

Hello Stat

According to the *International Listening Association**, 85% of what we know comes from listening, yet only 2% of professionals have engaged in any formal training or learning to improve their listening skills.

* I'm sure there may be a little bias in this research from the ILA, but you get the idea.

31

Social Media

The Colosseum of customer service

You're a Roman gladiator. You're standing in the middle of the Colosseum. The sun is blistering. Sweat's dripping down your back. Sword in hand. The crowd is going wild. The Emperor – looking ever so calm – has all the power. With a flick of his thumb, your fate is decided. Thumbs up? You live. Thumbs down? Let's just say it doesn't end well.

Now, fast-forward a couple of thousand years. We're not battling gladiators or lions any more, but we're still performing in front of crowds. Only now, the gladiators are you, your business, your brand and your customer service team.

The Colosseum?

That's social media.

And the stakes? Almost as high.

The Original Colosseum: Blood, Sweat And Sharks(!)

Before we get too deep into social mobs and thumb-ups, indulge me while I share a little history. The Roman Colosseum wasn't just some shabby stadium. It was the grandest arena of them all. Think Wembley's impressive? The Colosseum could hold 50,000 to 80,000 spectators. And these weren't your average football supporters, they were like Millwall fans – there for blood.

Gladiator fights were mainly man-on-man. But that was just the start. The Romans were nothing if not inventive when it came to entertainment. They flooded the entire arena for mock naval battles called *Naumachiae* (yes, millions of gallons of water in the middle of Rome!), sending ships out to wage war in front of a crowd that craved spectacle. There were wild animals; lions, tigers, even crocodiles. Some say they threw sharks into the water battles.

And the best part? It was free! The Roman emperors saw it as a way to keep the people happy and distract them from political issues. Food was often provided too, making it a grand day out. Talk about an early customer service experience!

After a day of snacks and spectacles, the crowd could influence the fate of the gladiators.

Thumbs up? Thumbs down? It was that simple. The emperor might've had the final say, but the crowd's roar certainly helped with his decision. Those thumbs carried weight.

And here we are, 2,000 years later. We've swapped the swords for smartphones and gladiators for brands. But guess what? The thumbs are still here. Only now, the digits are digital.

You create a post, craft an Insta or leave a comment on an article and within seconds… you're judged. A simple tap. Like or Dislike. Thumbs up or thumbs down.

Some things never change, just like in ancient Rome, the *crowd* has the power. It's not about whether your customer service was quick, clever, apologetic or efficient; it's about whether the crowd approves of your response.

Did you handle that criticism well? Thumbs up.

Did you mess up publicly? Well, I hope you've got thick skin because the crowd can be brutal.

The Psychology Of 'The Thumbs'

Crowdsourced justice comes into play when people 'thumbs up' or 'thumbs down' a post, comment, or brand. It feels exciting and reinforces our social validation (or rejection) instantly.

This type of public judgement is often a reflection of shared emotions. The thrill of the moment, or 'Mob mentality', where individuals are influenced by the emotions of the group. Often losing some, or much, of their moral compass.

Today, social media magnifies public judgement. The distance and anonymity of social media allows people to express their emotions without immediate consequences. Much like in the Colosseum, individuals may feel emboldened to give harsh feedback or 'pile on' a person or brand that's already being criticised.

Throw in a bit of confirmation bias and once a crowd starts leaning one way (booing a gladiator or panning a post), individuals within the crowd are more likely to follow suit and align their judgements to fit in and reinforce the collective opinion.

The Thumbs Of Today

What happens when you get a metaphorical thumbs down? A one-star review? Or public pasting? Maybe you've been hit by a viral post dragging your service through the mud.

The good news is it's not always game over. You see, in ancient Rome, a gladiator could sway the crowd. Even if the fight wasn't going his way, a perfectly timed act of courage or humility could change the outcome. The emperor's wavering thumb could turn.

On social media, you have the same opportunity. When you respond, how you respond, and most importantly, whether you're listening – is the modern battle.

Ripple Effect

In the Colosseum, winning wasn't always about defeating your opponent – it was winning the crowd. Gladiators were talked about then like we discuss rock stars now. Some even had sponsorship deals. Talk about personal brand!

Here are three ways to survive the crowd's thumbs:

Act Fast, But Don't Rush

In the anarchic amphitheatre, hesitation was death. On social media, speed matters. But rushing, without thought, will sink you faster. Take a moment, craft a genuine response – then hit send.

Own Mistakes

No one wins every battle. When you've messed up (and you will), own it. The crowd loves a bit of humility. Apologise, correct it and move forward.

Engage The Audience

Don't be afraid to engage, even when you're under fire. Show that you're listening, that you care and that you're human. The crowd might just throw you a lifeline.

In the end, social media – just like the Colosseum – is a public spectacle. You're judged in real-time. The crowd might love you today and hate you tomorrow. But remember, behind every thumb, up or down, is an opportunity.

It's not about winning the battle it's about winning the crowd.

32

Video Killed The Telephone

In December 2019 an average of 10 million Zoom meetings were held every day.

By March 2020 this had rocketed to over 200 million and, a month later in April, it had jumped to over 300 million daily Zoom events.

Phrases such as 'You're on mute' and 'Sorry, it's just the cat saying hello' became commonplace. Even my lovely mum, who struggles to use a mobile phone, was appearing in 'family Zooms' sharing poems, having a chat and connecting with family the only way we could.

Do you remember telephone conference calls? You could dial in from anywhere in the world and join a call with sometimes dozens of people. There could be a person on a train, in their car, or my favourite, a group of people at head office sitting around one of those strange starfish phones leaning in and desperately trying to understand what was going on.

Zoom changed that.

Unfortunately, users didn't realise the impact of video calls, what they can do for your reputation and how, when used correctly, they can be used for brilliant service.

A quick reminder. My definition of a customer is anyone who isn't you. So, this applies to colleagues, suppliers and anyone else who knows you. And it's never been more important to understand the adage – you only get one chance to make a first impression.

Here are 17 ways to make your Zoom* Zen.

Log In Early

The number of times people are late for a Zoom because the 'app was updating', or they simply couldn't log in boggles me. The Zoom app is always updating so check five minutes before to make sure that you are up-to-date.

Be Seen On The Screen

In large Zoom meetings the participants with their cameras switched on are noticed, remembered and referred to. I've participated in Zoom events with over 300 participants and only a dozen have had their cameras switched on. Those with their cameras on are prioritised to the first screen. The screen where the speakers and decision-makers are watching.

Looking good and being on that first screen is the modern equivalent of choosing to sit in the front row at a conference. Most people want to shuffle in and hide at the back. Don't be most people.

Be 'In The Room'

The temptation to multitask while participating in a Zoom call is as alarming as it is compelling. Imagine if you were in a boardroom or at an event, would you eat a bowl of cornflakes, play Candy Crush or do your eyebrows in the middle of the meeting?

I've seen people do all of those things. Even one session where a gentleman decided to remove his nose hair using his computer camera during the meeting. Memorable for all the wrong reasons.

* For the sake of simplicity Zoom can be Teams, Google Meet, Skype or any other video conference service.

Turn off email and other notifications that might distract you. Focus is critical on video calls. You may think you're being discreet, but people will notice if your attention is elsewhere.

Smile – Your Silent Superpower

Even if you're not speaking, your face can be seen by everyone on the call. Just think how important it is to have a genuine smile, be engaged with the camera and share some positivity.

Express To Impress

Facial expressions can speak louder than words, especially on Zoom. Nod when you agree, smile when appropriate and maintain an open, approachable demeanour. It shows you're listening and involved.

Prep With Purpose

Before the call, be clear on what you want to achieve. A little prep can go a long way – review any notes, questions, or objectives. When you know your purpose you'll steer the conversation more effectively.

Backdrop Basics

Ensure your background is clean and uncluttered. A messy, busy environment can be distracting. If possible, use a neutral or branded backdrop, or blur the background if necessary.

Let There Be Light

Lighting can make or break how you're perceived. Natural light from a window or a soft light placed behind your camera will brighten your face. Having a window behind you can make you look like an anonymous informant being interviewed for a TV documentary. Thinking 'cost per use', a decent light is a great investment.

Eye To Eye

Set your camera at eye level. This is probably the most important tip on this list and yet I'm astounded by the number of people on video calls where I've had to look at the top of their heads or into nostrils!

Eye contact builds connection, so when it's your turn to speak, train yourself to look directly at your camera – rather than at yourself or other participants on screen.

Silence Is Golden

Video calls can be noisy affairs. Mute your microphone when you're not speaking and know how to quickly (and that's the magic word!) switch it on when you are.

Just Drop It

If somebody has mentioned a document, a link or piece of information and you know exactly where to find it – copy it quickly and drop it in to the chat. A helpful way to engage without interrupting the flow.

Posture Power

Even though you're likely to be sitting down, how you sit matters. Sit up straight, keep your arms uncrossed and avoid fidgeting. A great way to help with posture is to dress as you would for a face-to-face meeting. You will sit differently.

Who Are You?

If it's a group call, introduce yourself clearly at the beginning – don't assume everyone knows who you are. This sets the tone and helps avoid confusion later on.

43 Minute Magic

Zoom fatigue is real, so be concise. Rambling not only bores others but can dilute your message. Plan key points to stay focused. In my book *How to Save An Hour Every Day* I suggested that the main reason most meetings last for one hour is because they're scheduled for one hour. A brilliant tip for a Zoom meeting is to schedule it for something like 43 minutes. That way you can be the hero when you gift everyone an extra 17 minutes of that hour by organising a shorter meeting that finished on time.

Use Visuals When Appropriate

Share slides, graphs, or even quick hand-drawn diagrams to illustrate your points. A bit of visual interest can break the monotony of talking heads and clarify complex ideas.

Seal The Deal

An immediate email summary of action points can reinforce what was discussed and ensure everyone is on the same page. It shows professionalism and helps with accountability. AI can do this for you!

Bring Energy

Zoom calls tend to sap energy compared to in-person interactions, so compensate by being more animated than usual. Smile more, speak clearly and don't be afraid to show some enthusiasm – it's contagious!

Video isn't going anywhere, so you'd better embrace it as it's going to become even more widely used. Your customers will expect you to be on video. Camera on, big smile, let's go!

33

The Power Of Names

Personalising emotional connections

You're in a crowded room and among the dozens of conversations you hear somebody say your name. Your ears prick up, your neural pathways fire and you're desperate to know who's talking about you.

Sciencey Bit

Psychologically, a person's name is deeply connected to their sense of identity and self-worth. Hearing someone use your name triggers parts of the brain linked to social bonding and positive emotions. So, by using someone's name in conversation, you are signalling that they are seen and recognised.

Names are more than labels; they're the essence of who we are. Using someone's name in conversation is a simple yet powerful way to show respect, build rapport and create a memorable interaction.

Dale Carnegie got it right: 'A person's name is, to that person, the sweetest sound in any language.' It shows you value and recognise them as an individual; a small act with a big impact, transforming routine exchanges into meaningful connections.

Hello Stat

According to a study by Epsilon, 80% of consumers are more likely to make a purchase when a brand offers personalised experiences, such as addressing them by name.

Here's a confession. I could be much better at remembering names. My wife, Christine, is brilliant at it. So good that sometimes (ok, often) I find myself nudging her and whispering 'Who's that?' Seconds later, fully armed and charmed, I can confidently greet the person and use their name.

Guess what? They don't know that I've just been briefed. And that's better than awkwardly searching for a name and missing a brilliant opportunity to put a big deposit in somebody's emotional bank account.

This isn't a book on memory tricks. There are some fantastic ideas in books and online that you can use to improve your memory – I must remember to read one. Techniques that will teach you how to recall somebody's name by using word association, repetition, memory hooks and a whole host of other ways to ensure you link that person with their name permanently.

When To Use Names:

Greeting And Farewell

Start and end your conversations with the person's name. It's a touch that personalises the interaction and makes it more memorable for both parties.

During The Conversation

Sprinkling their name throughout is like adding seasoning to the conversation. It keeps them engaged and signals that you're attentive and invested in the discussion. But like any seasoning, don't overdo it! You probably enjoy hearing your name, but not in every other sentence.

Acknowledging Contributions

Use their name when recognising their ideas or contributions. It reinforces their importance and shows appreciation.

Every Written Interaction

Start every email with a name, even in long threads. It's a small, respectful gesture. And remember, 'Hi Michael' is warmer than just 'Michael.'

Sciencey Bit

Research shows that hearing your name activates the medial prefrontal cortex, which is associated with self-perception and social identity. This activation reinforces emotional connections. And guess what? Hearing your name also triggers the limbic system, which processes emotions. This response explains why you feel positive emotions when someone uses your name – it taps into your need for social belonging and recognition.

What To Do If You Can't Remember A Name

Be Honest And Polite

If a name slips your mind, admit it gracefully. Saying, 'I'm sorry, I've lost your name, could you remind me?' is more respectful than just avoiding it.

Use Context Clues

Try to recall details about the person or ask for subtle hints. Context can often jog your memory. I know a brilliant bloke, Rodney Eccleston, who reintroduces himself to everyone and says where he's from. Even if you do know *his* name you instinctively reshare *yours*. If you don't, you still share yours and you hear his. Win/Win!

Repeat And Associate

Once reminded, repeat their name and create an association to help remember it for future interactions. Remember, there are whole books on this.

Hello Stat

Research from The Memory Institute indicates that repeating a name three times within a conversation can improve name recall by up to 80%.

Handling Difficult Names

Ask For Pronunciation

Don't shy away from asking how to pronounce a more challenging name. Most people appreciate the effort you put in to getting it right. See Chapter 3, The Cultural Lens, for more on this.

Practise And Confirm

Practise saying their name and confirm with them that you're pronouncing it correctly. This shows respect and a genuine effort to connect.

Use Nicknames – If Appropriate

If someone offers you a nickname or simpler version of their name, use it. But always take their lead. NEVER abbreviate without their consent. As soon as I receive any communication that starts 'Dear Mike', or I'm having a conversation where someone refers to me as 'Mike', they're immediately off my Christmas card list.

Ripple Effect

Using names correctly can create a ripple effect of positive interactions. It builds trust, shows respect and makes people feel valued.

Remember, a name is more than just a word; it's a gateway to connection and trust. Embrace the power of using names and instantly transform your interactions.

34

The Art Of The Greeting

One chance to make a first impression

First impressions are everything. Whether it's face-to-face, over the phone or in writing. The way you greet others sets the tone for the entire interaction. Making a great first impression should be simple, but it's full of nuances.

A well-crafted greeting can immediately create a positive atmosphere, establish rapport and set the stage for a successful interaction. A poor one is difficult to recover from and can set a telling tone for the rest of the communication.

The good news is, a few observations and tiny tricks can make all of your greetings great.

Face-To-Face

Let's start with in-person interactions. Give yourself a score out of ten for how good you are at meeting people face-to-face for the first time. If you gave yourself ten, skip this. But I bet you didn't. That's because we all know we could be a little better.

Here's a checklist. How many are you brilliant at?

Smile And Eye Contact

A genuine smile and direct eye contact convey warmth and confidence. They show that you're engaged and happy to meet the other person.

Firm Handshake

A firm handshake (not crushing) exudes confidence and professionalism. It's a simple gesture that can make a strong initial impact.

Use Their Name

Use the person's name and add a friendly touch. 'Hi Michael, it's great to see you!' This small effort can make the greeting feel more personal and sincere.

Check Your Breath

Ensure fresh breath. Keep mints or gum (get rid of the gum before the meeting!) handy. Bad breath will override almost all of your first impressions, undermining all the positive cues you're working to establish.

Check Your Appearance

Your appearance speaks before you do. Take a quick look in the mirror before meeting someone. Make sure your clothing is appropriate for the occasion and that you look neat and presentable. By showing respect for yourself you show respect for others too.

Practise Personalisation

Tailor your greeting to the situation. If you know something appropriate about the person or their preferences, use it in your greeting.

Posture With Purpose

Stand tall with your shoulders back. I know I sound like an army sergeant, but good posture exudes confidence and approachability. Slouching can make you appear uninterested or lacking in confidence. And walk with purpose. People unconsciously read body language and good posture with pace tells them you're alert and ready for the interaction.

Be Present

Distractions can derail an otherwise great first impression. When greeting someone, be fully present. Put away your phone or anything that might divert your attention. Show them they have your full focus. NEVER look over someone's shoulder.

Tone Of Voice

Your tone matters just as much as your words. A warm, welcoming tone sets a friendly mood. Too harsh or too soft and it might give off the wrong impression. Your tone should match the occasion – professional when necessary, but always approachable.

Respect Personal Space

Everyone has their comfort zone when it comes to personal space. Respecting that, particularly during an initial meeting, helps to ensure the person feels comfortable and not overwhelmed by you. This is especially true with handshakes – don't crowd, give them the space they need to feel at ease.

Telephone Greetings

People still use the telephone as a primary method to communicate. If I should call you, I would want you to use all seven of the ideas in this list to help me connect with you.

Clear And Cheerful

Answer the phone with a clear and cheerful tone. Your voice is the first impression, so make it positive and engaging. But please avoid 'singing' your greeting!

Identify Yourself

Always start with a clear introduction. In my office, we'd say, 'It's a brilliant day at Michael Heppell, [whoever] speaking. How can I help?' This sets our tone and lets the caller know who they're speaking to.

Active Listening

Show you're fully engaged by listening attentively and responding thoughtfully. Avoid multitasking during the call to ensure you're present in the conversation.

Avoid Hands-Free

Whenever possible, don't use hands-free systems. While convenient, they can create sound quality issues and make the conversation feel less personal. The caller may feel like they don't have your full attention if they can hear background noise or a distant echo. Always aim for the best sound quality and give the caller your undivided focus, holding the phone in your hand if possible.

Pace Yourself

The speed at which you speak makes a huge difference. If you talk too fast, the caller might struggle to keep up or misunderstand you. If you speak too slowly, it can seem like you're distracted or not engaged. There's a comfortable middle ground and you can usually find it by mirroring how your caller speaks.

Use The Caller's Name

As soon as you know the caller's name, use it appropriately throughout the conversation. See Chapter 33 on how using a name creates a more engaging and friendly experience. It shows that you're not just handling another call, but you're connecting with an individual. This simple act can help build rapport and make the caller feel valued, just as it does in face-to-face interactions.

End With Positivity

Just as important as the greeting, the way you end the call can leave a lasting impression. End with a polite and positive farewell – something like, 'Thank you so much for your call, have a brilliant day!' This leaves the caller feeling valued and ends the interaction on a high note.

Email Greetings

How many emails do you receive in a day and how many of those have a thoughtful opening line or greeting? Here are a few ideas to improve your emails.

Personalise The Salutation

Start with a personalised greeting. 'Dear Michael' or 'Hi Michael' is much warmer and more engaging than just 'Michael' or nothing. This simple addition shows you value the recipient.

Add A Friendly Touch

A few extra words can make your email feel more personable. 'I hope you're having a great day' or 'I'm excited to discuss this project with you.' Can set a positive tone.

Positive First Response

Always start with something positive, even if you've received a complaint. *Thank you for taking the time to write* is a great way to start building a positive conversation.

Match The Tone

Tailor your email's tone to the context and relationship. For a client or formal interaction, keep it professional but warm. For colleagues or casual conversations a more relaxed tone is appropriate.

Clarity In The Subject Line

Before the recipient even opens your email, they'll see the subject line. Make it clear and concise to set expectations and grab attention. A strong subject line is both direct and polite – think of it as the first step of your greeting. NEVER leave a subject line blank.

Acknowledge Previous Interactions

If you've previously communicated with the recipient, reference your earlier email or conversation. This makes the email feel more personal and connected. A simple, 'Following up on our last chat' or 'Great to speak with you last week' shows you value the ongoing relationship and keeps the communication fluid.

Thoughtful Sign-Off

End your emails with a considerate sign-off. 'Best regards' is better than 'Best', 'Yours sincerely' although old fashioned, in the right circumstances, is better than 'Yours'. Or why not develop a signature sign-off? I write 'Be Brilliant!' at the end of all my emails as it's on brand and adds a personal touch.

Face To Face

Responding To Common Greeting Questions

Most people don't think before they respond to questions. Instead, they go into *stimulus-response* mode where they give the same answer without really thinking about the impact that might have.

Here are some common questions and ways you may want to answer. These are just my ideas so it's worthwhile considering the questions you are asked regularly and how you might want to respond. Create a playbook and share it with others.

How Are You?

Instead of the usual 'fine' (the automatic response from 70% of the population) consider a more engaging response. I encourage saying 'Brilliant!' It's a positive, uplifting answer that often sparks curiosity and conversation.

What's New / What Are You Up To / What's Happening?

No one wants to hear, 'Not much'. Share something interesting or positive like, 'I'm reading a great book on customer service' or 'I'm working on an exciting project.' Say something that invites further discussion and shows you're open to sharing.

How Can You Help?

Be specific and proactive. Something like, 'I'd love to assist with your project. What's the biggest challenge you're facing right now?' Shows genuine interest and readiness to help.

Can I Ask You A Quick Question?

I get this one a lot. Instead of giving a generic response like, 'Sure,' use this as an opportunity to engage. 'Absolutely, what's on your mind?' This response opens the conversation while showing genuine interest and attentiveness. It encourages the person to ask without feeling rushed or like they're imposing on you. Sometimes, for fun, I'll say, 'Of course you can ask me a quick question. May I give you a quick answer?'

What Do You Think?

This can be one of those typical stimulus response questions where, to fill a gap, you respond without really thinking. At the *International Conference on Thinking* in Harrogate 2002, I asked Harvard's Dr David Perkins, 'What makes people brilliant?' He closed his eyes and thought on the matter while I, and a room full of eager thinkers, waited for what felt like an hour (it was probably 60 seconds) and only when he was ready, did he reply.

Do You Have A Minute?

Rather than just saying 'yes' or 'no,' offer a thoughtful response that acknowledges your time while still being helpful. For example, if it's with a colleague you could say, 'I'm in the middle of something, but I can give you five minutes now or we can have a more focused chat later – what works best for you?' This shows you respect both their time and your own.

How Was Your Weekend?

Instead of defaulting to 'It was fine', use this question to spark more engagement. How about something like, 'It was great, thanks. I caught up on some reading, visited a gallery and tried a new restaurant – how about you?' This adds a personal touch while inviting the other person to share their experience too.

NOTE: Please make sure you have been reading, visiting a gallery or trying a new restaurant or that answer is just weird.

The trick is to turn standard small talk into an opportunity for real connection.

Ripple Effect

The art of the greeting is more than the words you say; it's the impression you make and what happens afterwards.

Whether face-to-face, on the phone or via email, a thoughtful, personalised greeting sets a positive tone and opens the door to meaningful interactions.

You only get one chance to make a first impression.

35

Being Memorable:

The Hook That Sticks

Some people are naturally memorable. You meet them once and something about the interaction lingers. But being memorable doesn't rely on luck or charisma – it's about creating a hook that makes people remember you (in the right way) long after that initial encounter. A hook doesn't have to be grand or flashy, it can be small and subtle yet still incredibly effective.

The Builder Who Developed More Than Property

JC Walton (John Charles – but everyone called him JC) was a builder from Consett, County Durham. He wasn't known for his work; he was remembered for a habit that made him unforgettable. Everywhere JC went, whether it was a client's office or a project site, he left behind mints.

A mint became his signature. They weren't an afterthought; they were part of his identity. People associated mints with JC Walton. It was more than a detail, it was a tiny touch of thoughtfulness. It became his calling card, a simple, understated gesture that made him memorable long after he had left the building.

The best part? The mints weren't a sales pitch or a business card, he didn't have custom packs made with his business details emblazoned on them – they were Fox's Glacier Mints! But whenever someone found a mint, they thought of JC. It's over thirty years since I left Consett, but that still sticks in my memory.

Sciencey Bit

Small gestures that appeal to our senses (like JC's mints) create associative memory links in the brain. These links are formed in the hippocampus, which helps to store and retrieve emotional memories. Every time someone came across a Fox's mint, they were reminded of JC.

Why The Hook Works

The magic of JC's mints wasn't in their novelty – it was in their consistency. The hook doesn't have to be loud, but it does have to be repeated. JC didn't just do it once; he made it part of his routine. It wasn't just about leaving a good first impression, but about staying memorable long after he'd left the building.

So, what's your hook? What's the small, thoughtful thing you can leave behind that makes you linger in someone's mind? It could be a phrase, a story, a thank-you note or even something tangible like a mint.

The staff at Gran Meliá Hotels greet guests by placing their right hand over their heart with open fingers. This has an interesting cultural link to the language of 'Spanish hand fans', particularly within flamenco culture. In traditional Spanish society, fans were used to communicate subtly, often signalling feelings or intentions without words. An open fan near the heart signalled openness and receptivity, while a closed fan indicated rejection or disinterest.

So for staff at Gran Meliá Hotels it's a way to show their open-heart to guests. It's simple, traditional, memorable and free!

Creating Your Hook

Here's how you can develop a memorable hook that works for you:

Find Your Signature Gesture

Think about something that represents you or your business, something that reflects what you do or how you want people to think of you. It doesn't have to be expensive or elaborate. In fact, the simpler, the better. For some, it might be a signature phrase; for others, it could be a thoughtful follow-up action or a small token of appreciation.

Be Consistent

Just like JC's mints, your hook needs to be consistent. Repetition is key to making it stick. Whether it's in your emails, in-person meetings, or follow-up calls, make it a habit that people come to associate with you.

Keep It Authentic

Your hook must feel natural. It should align with your personality and values. JC's mints worked because it was a thoughtful and simple gesture that fitted his style. And he liked mints. If it feels forced, it won't have the same impact.

Think About The Lasting Impression

The goal isn't just to stand out in the moment – it's to leave a lasting, positive impression. Think about how you can enhance a customer's experience. Maybe it's leaving them with an insightful question or a useful resource. Whatever it is, make sure it adds value long after the interaction is over.

Make Them Feel Special

One of the most memorable things you can do is to make someone feel seen and valued. People may not remember what you did, but they remember how you made them feel. Whether it's a compliment, a thoughtful observation, or remembering their favourite coffee order, the details you remember and act on will help create a lasting impression.

Ripple Effect

A 2016 study by the Journal of Consumer Research, demonstrated that people are more likely to remember interactions that are emotionally charged, whether through humour, surprise, or thoughtfulness. The research found that emotional experiences create stronger and more vivid memories; meaning something like finding a gifted mint would be more memorable than a standard business card.

Here's another. My coaching client, Jonathan Bowman-Perks, has interviewed hundreds of incredible people for his *Inspiring Leadership Podcast*. At the end of every meeting, including the ones he has with me, he suggests, 'Let's share one thing to show appreciation for this time and each other.' It's a warm, wonderful and memorable way to reflect on the meeting and it's so much better than an action list.

Making Your Hook Stick

Being memorable doesn't mean trying too hard or going over the top. It's much more about consistency, being thoughtful, authentic and doing it in a way that leaves people feeling good about the interaction. Whether it's a mint or a heartfelt thank-you, the smallest gestures can become the most powerful of hooks. The ones that make people remember you for all the right reasons.

36

Don't Follow The Curve – Create it

Most organisations follow the curve. That's an exaggeration. Most don't even know there *is* a curve! You'll see that the majority look at what's already working and try to copy, do a version of, or, at a push, just do something a little bit better.

But the ones that stand out? They create the curve. They find a way to do something so unique, so impactful, that others scramble to catch up.

Ask *The Google* for ideas on leading edge customer service and you'll be given a bunch of examples such as *Apple's Genius Bars* and *Ritz Carlton's Empowered Employees*. They're great, but if you follow them now, you're just catching up.

What can you create?

It doesn't have to cost a fortune. Creating the curve isn't about being flashy. It's about solving problems in a way that may never have been done before.

Do you remember in 2012 when *Starbucks* started to write your name on your cup? They didn't invent this, but they did perfect it. And most customers loved it.

Creating the curve is about seeing opportunities where others see obstacles. And it always starts with one question: *What's missing here?*

Take *Octopus Energy*. They didn't just offer good customer service – they revolutionised it. When they couldn't find the software to deliver what they needed they created *Kraken*, which allows customers to track energy usage in real time, giving users control and transparency. It's a simple concept, but it transformed the relationship between provider and customer.

Then there's *Giffgaff*, the mobile network that's flipped the traditional customer service model on its head. Instead of call centres, they created a community where customers help each other in exchange for rewards. It's efficient, personal and builds loyalty in a way traditional telephone networks can't.

These organisations didn't follow trends. They spotted gaps and filled them with solutions no one else had thought of.

If you want to create the curve in customer service, start here:

1. Be A Problem Solver

Identify the frustrations your customers face – long queues, complicated processes, lack of clarity. Then ask, *How can we solve this in a way that no one else has?*

2. Anticipate Needs

Don't wait for your customers to tell you what they want. Study their behaviour, listen to feedback, then find ways to delight them before they even realise they have a need.

3. Empower Your Team

Great ideas come from those on the front line. Give your team the tools and freedom to make decisions that benefit the customer. Trust breeds innovation. And if you are on the front line, be brave and share your ideas.

4. Simplify The Experience

Customers don't want complexity. Whether it's making returns easy, streamlining a subscription process or using plain language instead of jargon, simplicity creates trust.

5. **Stay Curious**

Creating the curve isn't a one-off act. It's a mindset. *What can we do differently? What can we do better?* The moment you stop looking for the next curve, you start falling behind.

6. **Think Transferable**

How can you take something that somebody else is doing and transfer it into your process?

Creating the curve needs a little bit of daring. It's not easy and it won't always work. But when you get it right, you don't just stand out, you set the standard. And your competition? You'll be flattered when they start copying and following your lead.

37

Once Upon A...

A customer service manual might give you the right words to say. A training course could teach you the right actions to take. But if you want something to be remembered, tell a story.

People forget facts, instructions and corporate jargon. But they remember stories.

If you think about the best customer service experiences you've had, the chances are they weren't just transactions. They were moments that felt different, personal, or memorable. And they're easy to share because there is a story behind them.

Disney Traditions

I can't believe it's taken me this long in a customer service book to mention Disney. There's no one better at this. Disney doesn't just train its employees – they are immersed in stories.

Every new Disney Cast Member (employee) goes through *Traditions*, an onboarding experience designed to teach the history, values and culture of the company. But they don't do this by handing out dry manuals or with text-packed PowerPoint slides.

They tell stories.

Stories about how Walt Disney built an empire from a cartoon mouse. Stories about employees who have gone above and beyond to create magical moments for guests. Stories that make recruits feel like they're not just taking a job – they're becoming part of a legend.

This works because good storytelling creates connection, emotion and purpose. A Disney cast member doesn't just work at a theme park, they're part of the story.

The best companies (inside and outside of hospitality) use this same principle to create stronger, more engaged teams and share excitement and brand values with their customers.

The Balance Of Good Storytelling

Not all storytelling is good storytelling. There's a balance and this checklist will help.

Relevance

Great stories have relevance and they're 'on point'. Boring stories are rambling and at best have a tenuous link. They're the ones that might leave you thinking, 'eh?'

Interest

Brilliant stories, grab your attention. They make you think. You could listen to the storyteller all day. It's like time doesn't exist. We've all been subjected to boring stories; long-winded, irrelevant and self-indulgent. The ones that make you check your watch or wish you'd never asked.

Authenticity

When somebody speaks from the heart and shares a genuine believable story, you're hooked. In contrast, the wedge of doubt quickly sneaks in when you hear over-the-top, inauthentic, egotistical stories. You know the ones that sound exaggerated, pompous or just too good to be true.

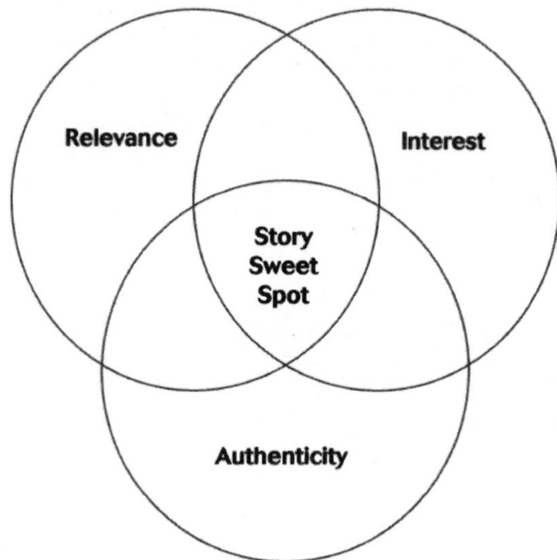

Great storytelling sits bang in the middle: honest, engaging and meaningful.

Using Stories To Enhance Customer Experience

Remember, your customers don't just want good service – they want connection.

The best brands don't just offer products – they offer stories that make their customers feel something.

Becoming Part Of The Story

L'Enclume, in the English Lake District, is an amazing restaurant. Not only do they tell you the story behind their ingredients, they invite you to be part of it. 'Our Farm' offers seasonal tours for diners so you can see where, and how, your food was grown, why their methods matter and how their passion for 'the perfect carrot' makes everything extra special.

Hello Stat

According to the Stanford Graduate School of Business, stories are remembered up to 22 times more than facts alone.

The Journey

A great story isn't just a sequence of events – it's a journey that moves the listener. And when a listener joins you on that journey, they'll feel something. That feeling creates connection, trust and engagement.

In customer service, stories shape how others see you. A business with great stories is a business people remember. Stories people hear about a company have a major influence (up to 65%!) on whether they buy, whether they return and whether they recommend it to others.

Stories have power. When you tell a good story, people stop and listen. And when they listen, they engage. In a noisy world a great story cuts through the chatter.

A good customer service story has four key elements:

Goal – Why are you telling it? A great customer service story isn't just entertaining – it serves a purpose, reinforcing what your brand stands for.

Grab Attention – Why should someone listen? The best stories hook you quickly with individual interest, clever connections or a solution to a personal problem.

Engage – Why care? Customers connect with stories that relate to their own experiences. *Newsflash* Even though you're the storyteller, you're not the most important person in the room. They are.

Enable Action – Why would they share it? A powerful customer service story is impactful and timeless.

Making Messages Stick

As a professional speaker, I use storytelling all the time. I could stand on stage and list tips, techniques and strategies for an hour. But I wouldn't receive many bookings or referrals. Or, I could tell a selection of stories that clearly make a point. Stories that the audience will remember and will inspire action.

And that's the key. People rarely remember information, they remember stories that made them feel something.

What's a signature story you could tell? It could be about the history of your organisation. A fun fact that's easy to reshare. Something about your product or service that makes you memorable.

Ripple Effect

> When you tell great customer service stories, you inspire others to create more of them.

Start Sharing Stories

This isn't public speaking. You aren't going to be judged. You don't need to follow a rigid storytelling formula. You don't need a marketing team to script the perfect brand story. You just need to start telling more relevant stories.

Instead of explaining a process, tell a story about how it helps individuals.

Instead of repeating a dry company history, share the magic moment that started it all.

Instead of reciting corporate values, tell a story of a time your team truly lived them.

To paraphrase the amazing Maya Angelou, 'People won't remember what you told them. But they will remember how you made them feel.' And stories are the key to creating that feeling.

38

The Power Of Positive Language

Words shape worlds. They can build trust, create warmth and turn an ordinary customer interaction into something memorable. And they can just as easily do the opposite – leaving people feeling ignored, frustrated or even disrespected. The difference isn't the message, but how it's being delivered.

Being Brilliant

I'm known as the 'Brilliant Guy', not because I'm necessarily brilliant, but because every time I'm asked, 'How are you?' I always reply with 'Brilliant!' In a world where most people say they are 'fine' or 'not bad' this stands out.

During my live events, I've challenged hundreds of thousands of people to ditch the 'Fine' and reply with 'Brilliant' for just 30 days. The results are amazing.

A simple shift in just one word instantly creates a different energy.

Positive language isn't about ignoring reality or being overly cheerful – it's about choosing words that uplift rather than deflate. In customer service, this means framing interactions with warmth and possibility rather than negativity and limitation.

Delivering Unfavourable News Positively

Not every customer conversation is easy. Sometimes, you must deliver bad news – a product is out of stock, a refund isn't possible or you have been delayed. The key is in how you say it.

People don't just hear words – they feel them. A simple shift in phrasing can turn a negative situation into one where your customer still feels valued and respected.

The Power Of Language In Communication

Research consistently shows that language influences emotions and perceptions. Studies in neuro-linguistic programming (NLP) suggest that the words we use don't just reflect our emotions, they shape them. When you use positive, solution-focused language, you not only make customers feel better – you feel better yourself.

Sciencey Bit

A study published in the *Journal of Positive Psychology* found that using optimistic language in conversations improves mood and engagement levels. Simply put, the way we speak affects both the speaker and the listener.

Vocabulary Size And Usage

The English language has over a million words, yet the average person only actively uses between 20,000 and 30,000. That means most of us are using just 2-3% of the words available to us.

When it comes to service, expanding your vocabulary – even slightly – can dramatically improve interactions. Instead of repeating the same standard phrases, introduce some dynamic and engaging language. Give your vocabulary an upgrade. And like any upgrade (and we all love an upgrade) it will make a difference.

For example:

Swap *'That's fine'* for *'That's perfect.'*

Swap *'No problem'* for *'My pleasure.'*

Swap *'I'll take a look'* for *'Let me find the best solution for you.'*

Words are tools. The more words you have in your toolkit, the better your customer interactions will be.

Using Positive Language As An Action

You'll often hear, especially in my world, that positive thinking is important. While I agree that positive thinking is good it's not nearly as important as **positive action**.

Imagine a customer leaves a review saying, *'The service was fine.'* That's neutral. But if they say, *'The service was fantastic, friendly and super helpful!'* that's a brand-building statement.

This is why every word you use matters in customer service. From the way you greet a customer to how you close an email, every word and phrase you choose is an opportunity to shape perception.

Practical Tips For Implementing Positive Language

If you want to instantly improve customer interactions, test these simple, but powerful techniques:

1. **Upgrade Common Phrases** – Replace neutral or negative phrases with more engaging alternatives.

2. **Slow Down And Smile** – The way you say something is just as important as the words you use. A positive tone can turn a simple response into a warm experience.

3. **Be Solution-Oriented** – Instead of focusing on what *can't* be done, always frame responses around what *can* be done.

4. **Practise In Everyday Conversations** – The more you use positive language in daily exchanges, the more naturally it comes into your customer service interactions.

5. **Listen To Yourself** – Pay attention to the words you use out of habit and challenge yourself to improve them.

Every word you choose in customer service has the power to either elevate an experience or diminish it.

Remember, positive language isn't about pretending everything is perfect – it's about shaping interactions with care, intent and optimism. When you master this skill, you don't just improve customer service – you create connections, build trust and leave a lasting impact.

Finally, 'How are you today?'

39

Feedback

The Gift You Didn't Ask For

Feedback is like receiving a Christmas present from a well-intentioned elderly aunt.

You open the package with anticipation. Maybe this year it will be something you'll love? Vouchers? Nope, it's fluorescent socks. Socks so bright they could land a plane. You'd never dream of wearing them, but what should you say to Aunty Betty?

Your aunt has taken the time to; choose something, buy it, wrap it and give it to you. And regardless of whether it's perfect or perplexing, there's an expectation. You smile, you say thank you and *then* you decide what to do with them.

Feedback is the same. Someone has taken the time to share their thoughts with you, whether via a quick comment, a detailed message or an in-depth review.

The first step in handling it is always to **say thank you.**

What happens next? Well, that's up to you. You might take the feedback on board and use it to improve.

Or, just like the fluorescent socks, you might decide it's not for you. And that's okay too – because, let's be honest, sometimes the customer is wrong. But just like you wouldn't tell your Aunty Betty her gift is awful, you wouldn't tell a customer that they're completely off the mark.

Why People Struggle With Feedback

Most people *say* they like feedback, but when it arrives, wrapped in a boxing glove, it can be a different story. Why do your defences rise when you're offered some 'constructive' feedback?

Ego Gets In The Way – No one likes being told they could do better, even when it's true.

Poor Delivery – Sometimes feedback is given in a harsh, blunt, or unhelpful way, making it hard to take on board.

Fear Of Criticism – Negative feedback can feel like a personal attack, making you defensive instead of receptive.

However, avoiding feedback means avoiding growth. The best organisations – and the best people – learn to not just receive it, but embrace it.

The Importance Of Feedback

Think about it like this: handled correctly, feedback is a shortcut to improvement. Instead of guessing what your customers want, they're telling you. Instead of assuming your service is brilliant, you receive real insights.

Hello Stat

77% of customers view brands more favourably if they proactively seek then apply customer feedback.

How To Gather Feedback

Some feedback lands in your lap. Other times, you need to go out and get it. Here's how:

Formal Methods

Net Promoter Score (NPS) – The simple question: *'On a scale from 0 to 10, how likely are you to recommend us?'* gives you an instant measure of your customer sentiment.

To work out your NPS, take the results of that simple question, then sort the responses:

> 0 – 6 are Detractors – not happy, and possibly telling others
>
> 7 – 8 are Passives – neutral, not complaining but not raving
>
> 9 -10 are Promoters – your biggest fans who will spread the word

Now, take the percentage of Promoters and subtract the percentage of Detractors. That's your **Net Promoter Score**. It's a quick but powerful way to measure customer loyalty.

Surveys – Short, direct questions work best. Long surveys are more likely to put your customers off.

Third-Party Research – This can be expensive, but for some organisations, using a professional research company is a great way to gather insight.

Feedback Forms - Make them accessible and easy to complete.

Informal Methods

Face-to-Face Conversations – Simply asking, *'How was your experience?'* can reveal valuable insights.

Social Media Listening – Customers often share feedback where they feel most comfortable – on their favourite platforms.

Observing Customer Behaviour – Watch what customers *do*, not just what they *say*.

How To Handle Feedback (Like A Pro)

The way you respond to feedback determines whether customers feel valued or ignored. Here's the right approach:

Listen Without Defensiveness – Even if it stings, take a few moments before reacting.

Say Thank You – Every piece of feedback, good or bad, is a gift. Acknowledge it.

Separate Emotion From Information – Focus on the message, not how it was delivered.

Act On It – If feedback is valid, make changes and let customers know you've listened.

Dealing With Online Reviews

Everything can be reviewed these days. If your business is on review sites such as Trustpilot you should always reply to critical feedback (if you have the time, reply to positive feedback too).

For a deep dive into handling online reviews, check out 'The Colosseum of Customer Service' see Chapter 31.

Ripple Effect

A single piece of well-handled feedback can transform a frustrated customer into a loyal advocate. A frontline team that embraces feedback becomes sharper, more engaged and more customer-focused.

Ignore feedback and the ripples fade. Act on it, and those ripples can turn into waves of improvement, loyalty and growth.

I get it, feedback isn't always comfortable. Sometimes, it's like getting the socks you didn't ask for, other times it's like a punch in the gut. But whether you use it, store it, or quietly move on from it, the key is how you receive it. Because the brands that listen are the brands that blossom.

40

Mastering The Follow-Up

Brilliant customer service in the moment is easy. A warm smile, a friendly conversation and a helpful attitude can make customers feel valued. But the real challenge is what happens *after* that?

Following up is where many fall short. They promise to call back and don't. They hand over an issue to another department and fail to check if it was resolved. They tell a customer they'll email an update but somehow forget.

And the worst part? As customers, we've come to expect it!

Hello Stat

80% of sales require at least five follow-up attempts after the initial contact, yet most businesses stop after just one or two. 27% of consumers say they never hear from a business after their first purchase, even though 81% are open to further communication.

These aren't just sales statistics – they reflect the reality of customer service too. Failing to follow up doesn't just leave a bad impression; it's a lost opportunity to build loyalty, trust and repeat business.

Why Follow-Up Matters

Following up isn't just a 'nice to have' in customer service – it's what separates the average from the exceptional. It does three critical things:

1. **Builds Trust** – When you say you'll do something and do it, customers feel they can rely on you. Trust is built through actions, not words.

2. **Shows You Care** – A simple follow-up email, or call, tells your customer they weren't just another transaction and they mattered enough for you to check in.

3. **Creates a Competitive Edge** – Because a follow-up is so rare, doing it well immediately sets you apart.

Think about it: how often have you been told, 'We'll get back to you.' only to hear… nothing? Following up is one of the easiest ways to exceed expectations, simply because most don't bother.

Examples

It's at this point that I would normally give a personal anecdote or example of a good or bad follow-up. This book has 244 pages and I fear I could fill them all… with bad examples.

In just one day this week, we experienced our TV Satellite provider saying they had sent a new box – it didn't arrive. My building society said they'll call back after 'talking to technical' – they never did. A delivery, I expected, planned my day around and chased – was abruptly altered to the following day with no reason given.

The issue isn't just the unresolved problem, it's the unfulfilled promise. And the worst thing? I wasn't surprised by any of those examples. That's how low the bar has been set.

These experiences highlight a major problem: businesses focus too much on *handing over* the problem and not enough on *owning* the solution.

Why We Have Follow-Up Failures

Most follow-up failures happen because of three things:

1. **Assuming Someone Else Will Handle It** – A customer's issue gets passed from one department to another and no one takes full responsibility for the outcome. I've experienced this in an organisation with two members!

2. **Not Setting Clear Expectations** – Customers are left waiting indefinitely because no one told them *when* they would hear back.

3. **Forgetting To Follow Through** – Without a proper system in place, follow-ups get lost in the chaos of day-to-day life.

What To Do – How To Master The Follow-Up

If you want to turn follow-up into your competitive advantage, here's how:

1. **Own The Outcome** – If you tell a customer you'll follow up, take full responsibility. Even if another department is handling it, check back to ensure it happened. Never assume.

2. **Be Specific With Timelines** – 'We'll get back to you' is vague. 'I'll call you by three tomorrow' is reassuring. Give customers a clear timeframe and stick to it.

3. **Use Systems, Not Memory** – Set reminders, use a CRM system, or just keep a notebook – whatever it takes to make sure no follow-up gets forgotten.

4. **Close The Loop** – Even if an issue has been resolved, a final check-in leaves a lasting positive impression.

5. **Surprise Them** – Follow up even when it's not expected. A quick 'Just checking if everything is still working well for you' can turn a one-time buyer into a lifelong customer and advocate.

Following up isn't that hard – it just takes some effort. It's the difference between a forgettable interaction and one that turns a customer into a loyal raving fan.

Let me challenge you. Think of a time when you were let down by a lack of follow-up. Now flip it – how can you make sure that never happens in *your* work? Good service in the moment is entry-level. Mastering the follow-up is the next level.

41

AI – Embrace Not Replace

AI is changing our lives more rapidly than we can keep up with. Whatever I write in this chapter today might (and probably will) be completely out of date by the time you read it. So instead of listing the latest tools or predictions, I'd rather focus on something more in keeping with the themes of this book. How to embrace AI without losing the human touch.

And if you want to know the latest AI trends? Just ask ChatGPT, do people still use ChatGPT?

Why AI Is A Game-Changer For Customer Service

AI isn't here to take over customer service – it's here to WORK WITH YOU to make it better. Used well, AI can:

Speed Up Responses – No one likes being put on hold. AI can handle FAQs, process simple requests and direct queries to the right place instantly.

Improve Consistency – AI doesn't miss the bus, suffer from lack of sleep, forget a name or have bad days. It delivers the same level of service 24/7.

Predict Customer Needs – AI can analyse patterns and anticipate a customer's needs before they are even aware. Loyalty 4.0 right there.

But the key: *AI should enhance service, not replace the human touch.*

The Right vs. Wrong Way To Use AI

This is just my opinion and it could change over the coming years or even months – scary. AI works best when it handles efficiency, leaving humans to handle empathy.

The Right Way:

Encourage the use of AI to answer basic customer queries while real people handle complex issues.

Let AI suggest personalised offers based on past purchases, but encourage humans to build relationships.

Use AI to automate routine tasks, freeing up customer service teams to focus on meaningful interactions.

The Wrong Way:

Replacing customer service with basic chatbots that frustrate customers.

Relying on AI to solve problems that require human judgement.

Removing warmth, personality and human connection from customer interactions.

Most customers don't mind speaking to AI, but they dislike the feeling that they're being passed around by an automated system that doesn't care.

Hello Stat

87% of consumers are comfortable using AI-enabled support via website chat.

What The Future Could Bring

My Dad ran a very successful roofing business. He was exceptionally talented and able to fix most roofing problems. I remember him proclaiming that robots would '*Never be able to put on a roof*'. I wonder what he would say now?

I asked my Artificial Intelligence Assistant (Brilliant Ai) if it was likely that robots could put on roofs. The results were fascinating, including this thought:

> A roofer doesn't just follow a script—they make real-time adjustments based on the shape of the roof, weather conditions and unexpected issues like warped wood or obstructions. A robot would need highly advanced AI with real-time decision-making capabilities, along with sophisticated vision and sensing technology to assess materials, detect hazards and place tiles or shingles with precision.

I found myself agreeing with my Dad. Robots would never (at least not in my lifetime) replace roofers or customer service experts. Here's why:

The Balance: AI + Humanity = Better Experience

I think we'd agree that people don't want more technology per se – but we do want better experiences. So rather than thinking about what AI *can* do we should ask: what do we *need* AI to do?

AI can track your orders, suggest solutions and manage bookings. But when something goes wrong? You want a human. A real person who listens, understands and can fix the problem with warmth and care.

Think of AI as your assistant, not your replacement. The organisations that get this balance right will lead the future of customer service.

What You Can Do NOW

You don't need a massive budget or a team of AI experts to start using AI in customer service. Here are three simple ideas you can test today:

Automate One Small Thing – Start with something simple: an FAQ chatbot, an AI-powered booking system or an automated email response. Test it, refine it and build from there.

Use AI To Personalise, Not Replace – AI can help you tailor experiences. Whether it's recommending products based on past purchases or using AI to craft smarter email responses, use it to enhance, not replace, personal connection.

Stay Curious – AI is evolving super fast. Keep an open mind, experiment with AI tools and stay informed. The best way to understand AI's potential is to use it.

AI isn't the enemy of great customer service professionals, it's a tool, that when used correctly, can make us even better.

Businesses that fear AI will be left behind. Those who embrace it, while maintaining human connection, will thrive.

42

How To Write So Readers Read

During the pandemic, I ran an online training programme called *Write That Book* – a course on how to write, publish and sell your book. Over 1,000 people took part, including more than 500 who signed up for one of six Masterclasses. During that time, I read a lot.

Some writers had a hypnotic way with words – whatever they wrote, you *wanted* to keep reading. Others? They lost me in the first paragraph. It wasn't the subject. It was the way they wrote.

The same applies to everyday writing. Whether it's an email, sales copy, a poster, a letter or even a social media post – the way you write determines whether people engage or switch off.

So, how do you write so your readers (your customers) read?

Start With The Reader, Not Yourself

One of the biggest mistakes in writing, whether it's a business email or a marketing campaign, is writing for yourself, not the reader.

You're not writing a novel. You're not writing to impress. You're writing to be read.

Customers don't care about how clever your writing is. They care about:

> *Is this relevant to me?*
> *Does it solve my problem?*
> *Is it easy to understand?*

If you start with the customer's needs, instead of your preferences, your writing instantly improves.

I love this lesson for writers:

> What's the purpose of sentence one?
> To ensure they read sentence two.

Readers make up their minds in seconds whether to continue reading or not. If your opening is dull, long-winded, or unclear... they're gone! Thank goodness you're still here.

Have you ever received something like this?

'I just wanted to reach out and follow up regarding the previous conversation we had where we discussed some potential options moving forward for your...

I'm already skipping to the end. How about something like this instead:

'Quick follow-up from our chat – here's an option I think you'll love.'

Less is more. Get to the point before they get bored.

Editing vs Writing – The magic often happens in the rewrite. Most bad writing isn't the result of bad ideas – it's often the result of bad, or no, editing.

The first drafts are messy. They should be. The key to great writing is rewriting.

In *Write That Book* I'd often suggest:

> Write first. Let it flow. Don't overthink.
> Edit later. Cut the fluff. Make every word earn its place.

One of my favourite tricks is to read out loud. If it sounds clunky, complicated or long-winded – it probably is. This is your chance to fix it before you press post, print or send.

What Would Your Grammar Say?

Poor grammar and 'creative' spelling is everywhere. I know language evolves, but that doesn't mean we should settle for sloppiness. Why risk annoying some of your customers because you don't know, and can't be bothered to check, the difference between 'there', 'their' and 'they're'?

Grammar checkers are FREE and accessible to everyone. Now that's a brilliant use of AI.

Tone & Style

Different messages need different tones. A formal letter, a friendly email, a marketing ad all have different styles but there are rules that apply to them all. They are...

Make It Easy To Read

Use short sentences. Long, rambling paragraphs make people switch off.

Ditch The Jargon

No one wants to read 'Synergistic Frameworks of Operational Excellence.' When you mean better ways of working together.

Jargon makes writing feel clunky, impersonal and harder to understand. Keep it simple.

Write How You'd Speak

If you wouldn't say it in conversation, don't write it that way.

Match Your Customer

And if you're not sure what tone to use? Match the customer's delivery. If they're informal, be informal. If they're corporate, keep it professional. Meet them where they are.

I like *Say This, Not That* guides.

Say: 'We'll fix this quickly.' *Not:* 'We are committed to expediting a resolution.'

Say: 'You'll get your order tomorrow.' *Not:* 'Your order is now scheduled for dispatch with an estimated arrival time within the next 24-hours.'

Say: 'Let's make a plan.' *Not:* 'Let's strategise a roadmap for execution.'

The simpler you can make your writing, the more people will read it.

The Danger Of Typos – Proofreading Matters

Even the best writers make mistakes. But failing to catch them can lead to serious consequences.

We've all seen some terrible examples of typos. There are bound to be some in your work, but thinking that your customers don't care, so you don't need to bother, would be a huge mistake.

Typos can damage your credibility and cost you customers. Always proofread your work – or better still, have someone else review it. Fresh eyes catch mistakes you might miss. Spotted any in here? Please let me know so we can fix them in future editions.

Sciencey Bit

Nearly 1 in 4 adults experiences reading fatigue after just 30 minutes of continuous reading. It's never been more important to have sharp and succinct writing.

By ensuring your writing is clear, concise and well-structured, you reduce the cognitive load on your readers, keeping them engaged for longer. And they'll thank you for it.

What You Can Do Right Now

If you want to write so readers read, here are some quick wins:

Cut the fluff
– If a sentence doesn't add value, delete it

Use the 'Read-Aloud' test
– If it sounds awkward, rewrite it

Put the most important info in first
– Don't bury key details in paragraph five

Format for skimming
– Use bullet points, subheadings and short paragraphs

Use a second pair of eyes
– A fresh perspective catches mistakes you'll miss

Great writing isn't about showing off. It's about getting your message across quickly, clearly and in a way that makes people want to continue reading.

And if you're concerned that you might be writing too much, it's ok to just stop...

43

How To Say No Nicely

In the world of customer service, the word 'no' can feel taboo. Some high-end hospitality businesses pride themselves on never saying 'no'. Yet, there are times when declining a request is not only necessary but also beneficial for both your business and your customers. The art lies in saying no gracefully, ensuring customers feel valued – even when their requests can't be fulfilled.

The Necessity Of No

There are scenarios where saying no is essential.

Pricing – Offering discounts to appease one customer can devalue your product and set unsustainable precedents.

Unrealistic Expectations – Some requests may be beyond your capabilities or outside of your service scope.

Fairness – Prioritising one customer's excessive demands can compromise the quality of service for others.

Boundaries – Not every opportunity aligns with your business goals and it's okay to decline those that don't.

Saying No Internally – The Hidden Challenge

Saying no isn't only relevant to external customers. Some of the hardest 'no' moments happen inside an organisation.

Think of a hotel reception area. The front desk team wants to offer outstanding service. But when they say yes to everything – late checkouts, dining requests, last-minute changes – there are consequences. Housekeeping struggle to service rooms. The restaurant is thrown off schedule because everyone wants a table at 8pm. New guests try to check in but now there are delays. What started as a yes to one guest, ends up causing problems for others.

The same thing happens in offices, retail and all other service industries.

A boss overloads an employee with work, expecting them to just 'manage it'.

A colleague asks for a favour that pushes your deadlines off track.

A client wants an urgent change, but the project team is already stretched.

The problem is people say yes to look good and avoid disappointing others. But that short-term win can create long-term issues. Perhaps you could reframe it like this: Saying no isn't always about being difficult, it can be about protecting quality, efficiency and fairness.

The Pitfalls Of People-Pleasing

While saying yes feels good and keeps people happy, excessive people-pleasing leads to broken promises, lost customer trust and team burnout.

Saying no isn't about rejection – it's about ensuring that when you do say yes, it really means something.

The Wrong Way To Say No

I may be championing saying no in this chapter but please avoid these common mistakes.

Being Blunt or Dismissive – This can quickly make your customers feel undervalued.

Over-explaining – Lengthy justifications can come across as insincere or defensive.

Avoidance – Ignoring a request, in the hope that it will just go away, damages trust.

The Right Way To Say No

Mastering the art of saying no means using the right tool at the right time. Here are a few scripts for your toolbox:

The Complimentary No: 'That's a great idea! While we are unable to offer that, here's what we can do…'

The Soft No: 'I would love to, but I'm unable to help on this occasion.'

The Solution-Focused No: 'Thank you for asking. We don't provide that service, but here's an alternative that could be perfect for you.'

Firm But Friendly No 'To ensure fairness to all of our customers, I'm sure you understand why we must…'

Charm And Confidence In Declining Requests – The Icing On The Cake

And finally here are a few flourishes to keep in mind when saying no:

Be polite but firm – Clear boundaries are respected.

Avoid over-apologising – A heartfelt simple, sincere apology will suffice.

Stay confident – A decisive no reduces ambiguity and the potential for further negotiation.

Ripple Effect

The 'Reverse' Ripple Effect

Sometimes saying yes when you should've said no can create a reverse ripple. Customers love to share with others what they managed to 'get away with'. Once two or three do this, you've inadvertently created a policy. I once saw this at an all-inclusive resort where branded drinks should've been extra. But the barman allowed a couple of guests to have premium drinks instead of the local offerings and word soon got around that for a dollar you could have what you liked. Ouch.

Knowing how to say no nicely is a vital part of effective customer service. When done with empathy and clarity it upholds your integrity and ensures that customers feel respected. Even when their requests can't be met.

A good no is like a traffic light – it might briefly stop the flow, but ultimately it's designed to keep everything moving smoothly and get you to where you need to be.

44

Communication In A Crisis

When things go wrong, and they will, customers don't expect perfection, but they *do* expect honesty. The way you communicate in a crisis can either build trust or destroy it.

A crisis doesn't have to be a major disaster, it could be something small like a missing product, a delayed delivery or you running late. Big or small, the rules are the same: customers appreciate honestly, clarity, speed and solutions.

Northern PowerGrid

I live in Northumberland and sometimes our weather can be, let's say, unpredictable. I'm always impressed at the way Northern PowerGrid handles crises – such as storms carrying an amber or red warning.

What makes Northern PowerGrid stand out for me isn't just the brilliant way they get homes and businesses reconnected, it's their excellent communication.

They don't wait for people to report issues then act – they actively prepare customers in advance.

Proactive Data Gathering – If you've previously reported a power issue to them, they retain your details and update you before the next storm even arrives.

Clear, Precise Updates – They tell home owners exactly what to expect: when power might go out, what they're doing about it and how long it could take to fix.

Multi-Channel Communication – They use maps, SMS, email, social media and even good old phone calls to reach customers, making sure no one is left in the dark (literally).

Practical Advice – They go beyond just reporting outages, by telling people what to do to prepare. Like having a torch ready, keeping freezer doors closed or keeping phones charged.

This approach reassures their customers, even in a frustrating situation, so they know what's happening.

The Crisis Communication Framework – A Three-Step Process

Whether it's a storm, delayed delivery or a customer complaint, great crisis communication follows the same three steps.

1. **Before The Crisis – Get Ahead Of The Problem**

    Most crises aren't *completely* unexpected. Identify potential issues in advance and prepare for them.

    Gather customer data and set up communication channels so you can send relevant updates.

    Identify weak spots – where could problems arise?

    Provide clear instructions in advance (be like Northern PowerGrid telling people how to prepare for a storm).

2. During The Crisis: Communicate Clearly And Consistently

Tell your customers what's happening as soon as possible – even if it's bad news.

Use multiple channels to ensure everyone gets the message.

Keep updates short, direct and useful – nobody wants a vague, rambling message when they just need to know what's going on.

3. After The Crisis: Learn, Improve And Rebuild Trust

Follow up with customers and thank them for their patience.

Be transparent about what you've learned and what you will improve next time.

Show that customer's feedback has been heard and acted upon.

Crisis Communication Isn't Just For Big Disasters

A crisis doesn't have to be a major event. Even small issues feel big to the customer experiencing them. The best organisations apply the same crisis communication principles, no matter the scale of the problem.

Product delays and stock issues – If something a customer has ordered isn't in stock, don't wait for them to chase you. Let them know asap, offer an alternative and be clear about when it will be available.

Restaurant substitutions – A great restaurant doesn't just say, *'Sorry, we don't have that.'* Instead, they offer a creative alternative, tell the customer immediately and make them feel looked after, not let down.

Missed appointments and running late – Life happens. If you're running late for a meeting or a job, let your customer know. A simple, timely heads-up builds trust.

Public transport – A message saying your train is running 15 minutes late due to signalling problems is easier to swallow than it being five minutes late with no explanation.

Bad Crisis Communication – What NOT To Do

When crisis communication goes wrong it creates confusion, frustration and long-term damage. Here are some mistakes to avoid.

Giving conflicting information – Customers checking social media, emails and phone updates should see the *same* message. Inconsistent messaging creates distrust.

Withholding the truth – Hoping customers won't notice an issue or waiting too long to admit a problem *always* backfires. Honesty – delivered well – builds respect.

Being vague or overly corporate – Nobody wants a robotic press release. Customers need clear, human responses. Empty statements like, *'We are experiencing some challenges and appreciate your patience.'* Will test said patience rapidly.

Ripple Effect

Communication, good or bad, doesn't just affect one customer – it's contagious. A single frustrated customer can leave a bad review, share their experience online or actively tell others not to trust you.

You can't always prevent a crisis, but you *can* control how you communicate during one.

When something goes wrong, your customers don't expect miracles. They just want honesty, speed, clarity and solutions. Whether it's a major power outage or a missing dessert, the best businesses use the same approach:

Apologise
Acknowledge the problem
Give clear updates
Offer solutions where possible
Check in and follow up

Use this approach and your customers may not forget the problem – but they'll remember how you handled it.

45

Learn The Language

When I was 10, I was part of an exchange group visiting Sweden and staying on the picturesque island of Björkö. I learned how to say *'Skynda dig, annars missar du färjan!'* well my version of it. For non-Swedish speaking readers it means, *'Hurry up, or you'll miss the ferry!'*

I wasn't trying to become fluent – I just thought it would be useful as my Swedish hosts said it ALL THE TIME. As it turned out, it became a kind of battle cry for the English group I was travelling with. Every time we found ourselves rushing for a boat, there it was, my one Swedish phrase, performed with gusto.

Looking back, I was probably shouting 'Turn the cabbage, it's the berry' or some such nonsense. But I quickly realised that I didn't need to be fluent. I just needed one memorable phrase, something that made people smile, that grabbed attention and made me feel a little more connected to the place I was staying.

And that's the point of this chapter. You don't need to master a language to make an impact – you just need to make an effort.

Why Language Matters In Customer Service

We live in a connected world. Whether you work in hospitality, retail, or any area of customer service, you'll likely interact with people from different, countries, cultures and backgrounds. A simple phrase in someone's native language can instantly break down barriers and create a more welcoming experience.

Imagine walking into a hotel abroad. The receptionist greets you in your native language with a 'Welcome back! How are you?' It's a small touch, but it changes how you feel.

Now flip it around. You're working in a hotel, restaurant, or shop and you've learned to greet someone in their own language. That shows respect, creates warmth and sets you apart.

It's not about perfection – it's about connection

Small Effort, Big Impact

You don't need to be fluent in Spanish, Mandarin or Arabic to impress someone. If you can learn just a handful of words, you can make a huge difference.

Here are a few that work everywhere:

Hello / Good morning / Good evening
Please / Thank you
My name is… / What's your name?
Welcome / Have a great day
Excuse me / I'm sorry / No problem
I'm sorry, do you speak any English?

That's it. Learn those in a few key languages and you'll be able to connect with people instantly.

The Role Of AI And Translation Tools

Google Translate and AI-driven translation tools can be game-changers. They allow you to communicate with your customers in real time, breaking down language barriers on the spot.

But here's the catch. AI translations are good, but they don't replace the personal touch. Reading something from a screen is fine. Spontaneously saying 'Welcome' or 'Thank you' in someone's language is better.

Use AI as a tool, but don't rely on it as a crutch.

Beyond Spoken Languages – The Power Of Sign Language

Not all language is spoken. British Sign Language (BSL) and Makaton are widely used, and even learning a few signs can make a world of difference to someone who is deaf or non-verbal.

Simple signs like hello, thank you, please, yes and no can transform how you interact with customers. Remember, just as with spoken languages, it's not about being perfect – it's about making the effort.

How To Learn Quickly (without wasting time on Duolingo)

Apps like Duolingo can be helpful – but only if you mix them with real-world experience. Otherwise, you'll just be on an '800 day streak' collecting pointless phrases about elephants and apples.

Instead, test this:

Set a goal: Pick a language that's useful to you (e.g., Spanish)

Use mnemonics: Create little stories or tricks to remember words.

Practise with real people: Customers will appreciate your effort, and they'll help and correct you.

Start with just five words and phrases: Don't overcomplicate it. Master five, then build on from there.

The best way to learn a language? Use it.

It's About Intent - Not Perfection

Here's your challenge: pick one phrase and four words in a language that interests you. Learn them. Use them. Watch what happens.

Now, *Skynda dig, annars missar du färjan!*

46

When Less Can Be More

Sometimes you don't need a lot of words to make your point.

47

The Craft Of Conversation

Most people think they're good at conversation. They're not.

Throughout this book, we've talked about the power of conversation and interaction – how it connects, engages and transforms customer experiences. But now, we're going deeper because great conversation is a craft. It's one thing to have conversations; it's another to master them.

The Biggest Mistake – Talking Too Much

A great conversation isn't about what you say, it's about how well you listen.

In my book *Flip It*, I share a story about a psychologist who took multiple flights between Los Angeles and New York. Instead of trying to be interesting, he focused on being interested. He simply asked great questions and let fellow passengers talk.

A week later, researchers contacted the people he'd sat next to and over 70% described him as 'one of the most interesting people they had EVER met'.

Think about that. He hardly spoke about himself. He didn't try to impress them. He just asked questions and listened.

People remembered him not for what he said, but for how he made them feel.

It's the key to mastering customer conversations.

The Power Of Questions

The best conversationalists aren't the ones with the most to say – they're the ones who ask the best questions.

A conversation dies without good questions. It either turns into a lecture (where one person dominates) or it fizzles out (because there's no engagement).

How To Ask Better Questions

Follow Curiosity

If a customer mentions something interesting, don't just move on – explore it. Curiosity deepens conversations and customer relationships.

> Guest: 'We're visiting for a special occasion.'
> Instead of 'That's nice,' ask 'Oh, amazing! What are you celebrating?'
>
> Client: 'We had a bit of trouble finding the place.'
> Instead of 'Glad you made it,' ask 'What happened? Where did you end up? Maybe you can help us improve our directions.
>
> Customer: 'I used to come here all the time.'
> Instead of 'Welcome back,' ask 'What's your favourite memory from past visits?'

Use Open-Ended Questions

Closed questions halt a conversation. Open-ended questions invite customers to share more.

> Instead of 'Did you enjoy your stay?' ask 'What's been the best part of your stay?'

Instead of 'Do you need any help?' use 'What are you planning to do today?'

Instead of 'Was everything okay with your meal?' ask 'What was your favourite course?'

Listen For What's Not Being Said

Sometimes a pause or hesitation reveals more than words themselves. Pay attention to tone, body language and gaps in the conversation.

A hotel guest says 'Yeah, the room is... fine.' That hesitation suggests something is wrong. Instead of moving on, ask 'Is there anything we could do to make it better?'

And if you get a short answer, follow up.

For example, if they say, 'No, it's ok'.

Follow up with, 'We don't like ok, if there was one thing that would make it better, what might it be?'

A customer says 'It was an interesting experience.' That could mean good or terrible. Clarify with 'I'm intrigued. Why was it interesting?'

A team member says 'I'm doing okay, I guess.' Instead of leaving it there, show you care: 'I noticed you paused – how are you really?'

Reflect And Confirm

Show you're truly listening by reflecting and feeding back on what you hear. This builds trust and makes customers feel heard.

'So what I'm hearing is that the order process felt a bit clunky. Is that correct?'

'You mentioned you had a problem with delivery – please can you tell me more, so that we can fix it?'

Give Permission To Share More

Some people won't open up unless invited. Simple phrases encourage them to continue and expand.

'Take your time, I'd love to hear more about that.'

'That sounds important, can you tell me more?'

'I don't want to assume. Tell me, what would be most helpful for you?'

Ask, Listen, Respond

If you want to transform your customer conversations, use this simple three-step approach:

Ask – Start with a great question.

Listen – Truly hear what the customer is saying (don't just wait for your turn to speak).

Respond – Acknowledge, add value and keep the conversation going.

Is this patronisingly simple? Maybe, but the next time you're having a conversation observe the flow. It's simple – but wow it's powerful.

Bad Conversation Habits To Avoid

If you want to master customer conversations? Stop doing this:

Interrupting – Cutting people off kills connections

Making it about you – *'Oh, that happened to me too...'* isn't helpful

Filling silence – Pauses aren't awkward – they're an opportunity for brains to catch up

Giving one-word answers – Conversations need flow

Make Customers Feel Heard

The best conversations aren't about saying the right thing. They're about making the other person feel valued and heard.

If you can master asking better questions, listening more than you talk and responding with care, you won't just have great customer conversations, you'll build trust, loyalty and unforgettable experiences.

Ripple Effect

Colleagues who feel listened to are more likely to listen too.

48

Why Should I Use You?

Imagine you're a plumber. You may think your competitors are other plumbers – but they're not. These days your biggest competitor is DIY, followed by customers ignoring their problem (let it drip!) and finally choosing a cheaper option.

In a world where you can book your own global travel, order anything at the tap of a screen you can also learn plumbing from YouTube tutorials. So why should anyone use a travel agent, visit a shop or have you clamber under their sink?

It's Not About Price, It's About Value

Your biggest challenge isn't just standing out – it's proving why using *you* should be the natural choice. If price were the only factor, every industry would be in a race to the bottom. That's not a race you can win. You need to be in a different fight. The battle to be worth it.

Because value beats price – every time.

Value is made up of three things:

Outcome – How does it solve the problem and will it last?

Experience – Is it easy, enjoyable and stress-free?

Extras – What unexpected benefits make you stand out?

When you create value, people will readily pay more without shopping around and without questioning every penny. The emotional brain makes the decision and the logical brain justifies it. And giving value covers both.

You Can't Claim Value – You Have To Prove It

Anyone can say, 'We're the best.' It means nothing. In a world where people can read reviews in seconds and fact-check everything, empty claims are quickly exposed.

Four Ways To Prove Your Value

Authenticity First – Believe In What You Do

Customers can smell insincerity. If you don't genuinely believe in your product or service, why should anyone else?

Start with what you know or do brilliantly. Maybe you offer:

High-quality craftsmanship

A timely, stress-free experience

A superior level of care

Whatever it is, own it. Be proud of it and *then* communicate it. But do it like this.

Let Others Speak For You - The Power Of Testimonial

The most powerful marketing isn't what *you* say – it's what *others* say about you.

Reviews, word-of-mouth and referrals matter more than ever. As consumers, we are becoming more exposed to a world of fear, a world where we are encouraged to trust less and doubt more. There's a vacuum. Customers are desperate to find someone they can have confidence in. They're crying out for someone to trust. So make it easy for them. Filling the vacuum and make yourself the one to trust.

> Do your customers leave glowing reviews? Share them.
>
> Have past clients told you they'd recommend you? Ask them to.
>
> Have you transformed someone's experience or life? Write a case study.

The key is to build a reputation so strong that your customers advocate for you.

Demonstrate It – Show, Don't Tell

Saying, 'We do high-quality work' is just talk. Providing before-and-after photos or videos, sharing real results and offering guarantees – that's proof. When your customers advocate, that's social proof.

The clearer your proof, the easier the decision.

Be Consistent – Build A Reputation

One great experience is nice, but it's a history of great experiences that builds trust. People return to businesses that do what they say they will do. Then prove it again and again and again.

Be honest:

> Do you follow up when you say you will?
>
> Do you deliver on your promises? Not just sometimes, but always?
>
> Do customers come back, not because they have to, but because they want to?

Consistency turns one-time buyers into lifelong advocates.

Your Challenge

Lots to think about, but thinking isn't enough. Now it's time to act.

Write down three reasons why someone should choose you over DIY or a competitor.

Then ask, how can I demonstrate this?

The organisations that thrive are not the ones that claim to be different. They're the ones that show it.

49

Your Customer Service Brand

What is a brand? For some, it's a logo. For others, it's a catchy tagline or a slick website. But a brand is far more than any of those things.

A brand is the sum of all that you do, how you do it and how you make people feel. It's every interaction a customer has with your business, from the way they're greeted to how quickly you solve their problems. In short, I believe *your service is your brand.*

Disney: The Gold Standard Of Customer Service

Disney is, without doubt, one of the best examples of a brand that lives and breathes customer service. From the moment you step into one of their parks, every single detail reinforces their promise of 'magic.'

What sets Disney apart is the consistency of their service. Every employee, from ride operators to janitors, is trained to deliver an exceptional customer experience. It doesn't matter whether you're buying a ticket, meeting Mickey Mouse or asking for directions – Disney makes you feel like their most valued guest.

What's remarkable about Disney Theme Parks is their ability to embed their brand into every interaction. And this is not accidental – it's intentional.

Rate The Brand

When we run our *Hearts and Minds* workshops, we have a '*Sizzle Session*' called *Rate the Brand*. In small groups, participants are given 10 cards with the logos of well-known brands and they are asked to rank them from 1 to 10, from best to worst, based on their opinion of the customer service brand.

Some, like Disney, consistently land at the top. Others, like HMRC, might appear near the bottom. What's interesting is that some brands, like Ryanair, are comfortable with this. Their business model isn't built around exceptional customer service and they don't pretend it is. They've chosen cost-efficiency over service and their brand reflects that. At least they're honest.

The fascinating part of the exercise comes when participants are given one more card featuring their own logo and they're asked to rate their brand. Many hesitate to put themselves at the top because they don't believe they are 'the best.' At the same time, they don't believe they are the worst. They aim for the middle. But here's the problem: nobody remembers the brands in the middle.

If you want your service brand to stand out, you can't settle for average. You need to be brilliant.

Common Branding Mistakes

Here are some pitfalls to avoid when building a brand:

Thinking It's Just A Logo

A beautiful logo won't save you if your service doesn't match the image you're projecting. Customers care much more about how they're treated than your choice of font.

Inconsistency

If one branch of your business delivers stellar service but another falls short, it weakens your brand. Consistency across the brand builds trust.

Overpromising, Underdelivering

Flashy slogans like 'World-Class Service' fall flat when the experience doesn't live up to the hype. Be realistic and ensure you're ready to deliver on what you promise.

Forgetting The Human Touch

Automation and efficiency are important, but nothing beats the warmth of human connection. Robots don't build loyalty – people do.

Making It Too Complicated

If I ask for your mobile phone number you can probably recite it without thinking. If I were to ask you to say your mobile phone number backwards, it's hard. Your brand should be easy to recognise, easy to understand and easy to engage with.

If you want to make sure your customer service reflects your brand, here's where to start:

Empower Your Team

Train everyone so that they understand your brand values. If you're an employee and you don't know your brand values, ask. Ensure everyone has the autonomy to make decisions that align with those values.

Be Consistent

From tone of voice to how you handle complaints, ensure your service feels the same across all touchpoints – whether online, in-store, in print or on the phone.

Does The Experience Match The Brand Promise?

Ask yourself, *If our customer service was the only thing a customer experienced, would they still recognise our brand?*

Dive Into The Details

Great service brands are built on detail. You could be dropped into an Apple Store anywhere in the world and you would know instantly where you were and what to expect.

Harvest Feedback

Regularly ask your customers if your service is matching their expectations. Their insights will help you to fine-tune your brand experience.

I do love logos. But remember, your logo is just a visualisation of a promise. It's the service you deliver every day that turns that promise into reality. If you want to build a strong brand, don't just focus on how your business looks – focus on how it *feels*.

50

Build Your Bridge

This is it. The final chapter. The moment when you decide whether *See, Smile, Say Hello* is just another book for your shelf, or something that will transform how you deliver customer service.

At the start of this journey I shared a simple framework:

See your customer before they see you

Smile at your customer before they smile at you

Say Hello to your customer before they say hello to you

If that's all you take away, you'll already be in the top 5%. But if you want to go further, to deeply embed these ideas, then think of your customer service like a bridge. A bridge that connects you to your customers, builds loyalty and stands the test of time.

Laying The Foundations – Trust

A bridge isn't built overnight. It starts with strong, deep foundations – just like great customer service starts with trust.

Trust isn't something you demand from your customers; it's something you earn. Every interaction, every decision, every moment where you choose to do the right thing (even when no one's watching) cements that foundation.

Without trust, there is no bridge.

The Supporting Pillars – See, Smile, Say Hello

Every great bridge is held up by solid pillars. *See, Smile, Say Hello* are yours.

They're more than a catchphrase, they hold everything together.

See – Anticipate your customer's needs. Be aware of how they feel, what they might need and how you can make their experience outstanding.

Smile – The fastest way to create an emotional connection. Not with a grin, but a genuine smile from the heart that makes customers feel welcome and valued.

Say Hello – Communication is everything. It starts with a greeting but extends to listening, engaging and responding with genuine care.

There are three principles – you can't choose two favourites, you must commit to all three. They're the structure that supports your bridge, especially under pressure.

Handling Pressure – When Things Go Wrong

Every bridge faces stress – bad weather, heavy loads, unexpected events. Your customer service will too.

Customers will be rude. Demands will be unreasonable. Things will go wrong.

But the best don't collapse under pressure – they flex, adapt and respond with calm confidence and clarity.

When there's a complaint you'll see it, acknowledge it and act fast and appropriately.

When a customer demands more you'll smile, be professional and be perfectly personable.

When things don't go to plan you'll communicate quickly, clearly and honestly.

A bridge doesn't waver in a storm. It holds firm.

Maintaining And Strengthening

Even the strongest bridge needs maintenance or it will weaken and collapse.

Brilliant service is no different. It's not something you 'set and forget.' Service is something you train, refine and improve.

Daily conversations about service keep standards high.

Small improvements prevent bigger problems from occurring.

Listening to feedback helps you fix weak spots before they become major cracks.

The best customer service teams never stop improving.

Crossing Over

A bridge isn't only about engineering and aesthetics, it's there to be used. To make life easier, smoother and convenient for those who need it.

Service is the same. If all you do is read this book but take no action, then nothing changes,. But if you apply what you've learned, test the ideas and commit to change, you'll create something lasting that connects people, builds loyalty and makes a lifelong difference.

Now it's over to you.

Build your bridge.

I can't wait to See, Smile and Say Hello to you soon.

Acknowledgements

First up, without doubt, you would not be holding this book and have read this far if it wasn't for... drum roll... the brilliant Christine Heppell. Not only does she make sure I function as a happy human, but she also ensures you can read this book without thousands of mistakes, wasted words (seriously she probably chopped out 25%) and pages upon pages of self-indulgence. Thank you Christine – I love you with all my heart (I know you'll try and cut this bit out, but it's staying).

The beautiful typesetting and the fact that your eyes aren't feeling tired or distracted is down to the brilliant Matt Bird.

Sarah McGeough spent two years working as my project manager and was instrumental in keeping me on track during the developmental stages of this project.

Vanessa Thompson is my brilliant Personal Assistant who always makes me better!

Thank you to all the amazing organisations who exemplify brilliant customer service. We learn from you, are inspired by you and share your best ideas and practises.

Without feeling fit, energised and healthy, there's no way I could do what I do. We have an amazing team of people who help us to keep our energy levels high and our health on point - they include Dr Guillermo Recatero, Dr Fiona Ellis, Dr Naresh Lakhwani, Dr Martha Macías Sánchez, Sam Peterson, Sergio

Recatero, the team at Buchinger Wilhelmi and a whole bunch of other therapists and specialists. Thank you.

Thank you to all the wonderful people who are connected with me and follow me on social media. I love your suggestions, likes and comments and I especially like it when you let others know that I have a new book out. Heavy hint!

You'll see this book is dedicated to my best mate Andy Alderson. Andy lives and breathes brilliant customer service.

About the Author

Michael Heppell is the International Best-Selling author of 9 books. His personal development and business books have been published in 29 languages and are available in over 80 countries.

Michael is a popular keynote speaker who's been described as one of the top three professional speakers in the world.

As a coach, he's helped everyone from TV presenters to Premiership footballers, new authors to seasoned professionals.

www.MichaelHeppell.com

More Books by Michael Heppell

If you've enjoyed See, Smile, Say Hello you'll enjoy Michael Heppell's other books:

How to Be Brilliant:
Change Your Ways in 90 Days!

How to Be Brilliant provides powerful strategies to help you move from average to brilliant as quickly as possible with as much fun as possible.

5 Star Service:
How to Deliver Exceptional Customer Service

5 Star Service delivers 100+ tips and strategies to delight customers, outshine competitors and drive repeat business.

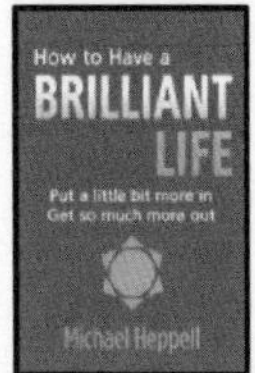

How to Have a Brilliant Life:
Put a Little Bit More In Get So Much More Out

How to Have a Brilliant Life helps you focus on what matters, make lasting changes and create your best possible life

Flip It: How to Get the Best Out of Everything

Flip It - How to get the best out of everything shows you how to switch your thinking, overcome challenges and get the best from every situation.

How to Save an Hour Every Day:
Guaranteed

How to Save an Hour Every Day offers simple, powerful strategies to beat procrastination, streamline tasks and reclaim your precious time.

The Edge:
How The Best Get Better

The Edge by Michael Heppell reveals the habits and mindset of top achievers, helping you unlock success and continuous improvement.

17: Your Ultimate Guide to a Better, Brilliant You

17 shows you how to unlock success through 17-minute sprints, 17-day projects and 17% improvements for maximum productivity and achievement.

Write That Book:
How to Write, Publish and Sell Your Book

Write That Book by Michael Heppell is a step-by-step guide to writing, publishing, and selling your book, turning your dream into reality.

If you would like to connect, enjoy reading some bonus chapters, receive a weekly newsletter and discover more about Michael visit www.MichaelHeppell.com.